NANTUCKET SLEIGH-RIDE

A Notebook of Nautical Expressions

Rock Village Publishing
41 Walnut Street
Middleborough MA 02346
(508) 946-4738

Other books by Edward Lodi

Deep Meadow Bog:
Memoirs of a Cape Cod Childhood

Cranberry Chronicles:
A Book About A Bog

Forty-one Walnut Street:
A Journal of the Seasons

Cranberry Gothic:
Tales of Horror, Fantasy, and the Macabre

Shapes That Haunt New England:
The Collected Ghost Stories of Edward Lodi

Haunters of the Dusk:
A Gathering of New England Ghosts

The Haunted Pram:
And Other True New England Ghost Stories

The Haunted Violin:
True New England Ghost Stories

Murder on the Bogs:
And Other Tales of Mystery and Suspense

Ida, the Gift-Wrapping Clydesdale:
A Book of Humorous Verse

The Ghost in the Gazebo:
An Anthology of New England Ghost Stories
(editor)

Witches of Plymouth County:
And Other New England Sorceries

Witches and Widdershins:
A Modern-day Witch Story

The Old, Peculiar House:
Ghost Stories Read by the Author
(one-hour audio on CD)

NANTUCKET SLEIGH-RIDE

A Notebook of Nautical Expressions

ROCK VILLAGE PUBLISHING
MIDDLEBOROUGH, MASSACHUSETTS

Nantucket Sleigh-Ride
Copyright © 2005 by Edward Lodi

Original oil painting "Nantucket Sleigh-Ride"
Copyright © by Robert Duff

Typography and cover design by Ruth Brown

ISBN 0-9721389-9-4

This book is dedicated to
ROBERT DUFF
the artist whom I most admire.
His paintings *are* New England.

"There never was a very great man yet who spent all his life inland. A snuff of the sea, my boy, is inspiration; and having once been out of sight of land, has been the making of many a true poet and the blasting of many pretenders; for, d'ye see, there's no gammon about the ocean; it knocks the false keel right off a pretender's bows; it tells him just what he is, and makes him feel it, too. A sailor's life, I say, is the thing to bring us mortals out."

—*Herman Melville,* White-Jacket

Preface

For purposes of this book, the term "nautical expression" encompasses more than one definition. It refers to a slogan or phrase that may once have been current among sailors, but which is now long obsolete; it equally applies to a word or phrase commonly used today in everyday speech, but whose origin can be traced to our seafaring heritage.

Growing up on Cape Cod I became aware at an early age of New England's rich maritime history. I was less aware at the time of the influence of that history on the spoken (and written) language, though I remember distinctly, as far back as the 1940's, certain nautical terms that were used on the cranberry bogs, where my father was foreman and where, at harvest time, my mother was also employed, as tally keeper and later in the season as a screener. I spent many a carefree day on the bogs, playing at the edge of the ditches, hunting turtles and frogs, or helping the harvesters by fetching empty boxes for them to fill, or passing along a dipper brimful of cool water from the communal can conveniently stored in the shade.

The empty boxes were stacked in pyramid-shaped piles on *shore*.

Now, for those not familiar with the culture of cranberries I should point out that although the berries are grown on "bogs" (in Massachusetts; elsewhere, in Wisconsin for example, they're sometimes called marshes), "fields" might be a more accurate term. The early cranberry growers planted vines in swampy areas that were formerly bogs (often where bog iron had been mined) but which were, essentially, drained. "Sunken fields surrounded and intersected by irrigation ditches" would be an apt description. Back in the days when cranberries were picked by hand or scoop (and later by machines), the bogs had to be absolutely dry before harvesting could begin. For the most part, during harvest season the "bogs" with their plush carpet of vines were hot and dusty. There was a cranberry bog near the house where I lived on which—much to the chagrin of the hapless owner—impromptu games of baseball were sometimes played by summer residents of the area who were oblivious to the field's true nature, and to the damage they were doing to the potential crop.

The upland area immediately surrounding the bogs was referred to as "shore" for a simple reason. The first cranberry cultivation was begun—on Cape Cod in the early nineteenth century—by retired sea captains. It was natural for those **old salts** to use terms with which they were familiar. To them, metaphorically, the bogs were tiny seas, and the bordering land, the shores of those seas. Likewise, the irregular sections of bog that extended from the main body into the surrounding upland were referred to as "bays." Flat areas of upland adjacent to the bogs (used for stacking boxes or unloading equipment) were sometimes called "islands," especially by the old-timers.

I seem to remember—though at this great distance in time I cannot be sure—that many of the knots used on the ropes to secure the loads of boxes of empties or harvested berries on the trucks had nautical names. By the time I was tying those knots, in the 1950's and '60's, I had forgotten their names and knew only their purposes. But at least I could honestly claim that I **knew my ropes**, a nautical expression tried and true, still very much in use here in the twenty-first century.

The influence former sea captains had on the language extended to all areas of life. In *A Pilgrim Returns to Cape Cod* Edward Rowe Snow, writing in 1946, tells of an old salt acting as usher at the local Methodist church. Greeting visitors from out of state, he asked, "Where would you like to sit—forward, aft, or amidships?" And in his book of memoirs of a life at sea, *Fair Winds & Foul*, Frederick Perry offers up this description of a prizefighter turned sailor: "His starboard ear was cauliflowered and spread out on the side of his head, his nose was twisted athwart-ships and his face was an exact reproduction of a terra-cotta bulldog."

In the nineteenth century, the propensity of sailors to use nautical terms while ashore was well known. The wife of one captain, who accompanied her husband on a voyage in 1837, recorded in her journal (quoted by Joan Druett in *Hen Frigates*): "By this time I had learned all the nautical phrases, though I did not choose to use them, lest I get in the habit, and use them on shore, which would be very mortifying for a captain's wife."

Some of the words and phrases of nautical origin which I've chosen to include in this little notebook are obsolete, nowadays seldom if ever heard in speech and encountered occasionally only in books the writing of which predates a certain era. **Back and fill**—with the meaning of "to act indecisively"—is, I suspect, such an expression. Others like **dead beat** have not lost their currency—are still very much in use, in fact. Others fall somewhere in the middle; they're familiar to some, unknown to others.

Son of a sea cook may fall into that latter category. Back in the 1960's—my poker-playing days—the father of one my friends, who would sometimes join us in our all-night poker sessions, was fond of the expression. When chagrined at the cards he'd been dealt, or the outcome of a game, he'd exclaim, "Son of a sea cook!" If his wife was present she'd admonish him with "Charles!" and a stern look, and he'd know it was time to clean up his language. I should add that he was a man of the sea, fond of fishing; at the time I knew him he ran a boat livery on the Weweantic River. Nautical terms came natural to him. In these days when four-letter words are freely mouthed in public, **son of a sea cook** no longer serves as a euphemism for a slightly stronger utterance. It's used humorously, if at all.

Although I once taught English at the Massachusetts Maritime Academy in Buzzards Bay—on the very edge of the Cape Cod Canal—I lay no claim to a maritime background other than the fact that I grew up on Cape Cod (surrounded as it were by water)—which may be one reason why my career at the Academy lasted but a few scant years. Ah, but I do lay claim to a rollicking love for the English language, along with some expertise in it, hence this little collection of verbal nautical odds and ends.

"Odds and ends" is the key phrase. By no means is this book intended to be exhaustive. More has been left out than has been included. There are a number of reasons for this. Space, for one thing. This is a mere chapbook, for goodness sake, not an encyclopedia. Indeed, without exaggeration, it would take a tome the size of an average dictionary just to include all the words and expressions that are or have been in use on the high seas, along the shores, or in everyday speech, which owe their origin to ships and the sea. For instance the word *aloof*, meaning "socially distant," derives from an obsolete nautical expression that refers to steering a ship up into the wind. It is only one of many hundreds of terms that might have been included, had time, space, and patience permitted.

I've omitted some material because it's too obvious to need inclusion. The expression, "deep and wide," for example, with the colloquial meaning of "thoroughly and exhaustively." To anyone who hears it or sees it in print the meaning and provenance should be no secret. We are, after all, talking about the ocean. And what is the ocean if not deep and wide?

Then there's the other extreme, expressions that were once common but are no longer found in ordinary speech. "Hannah Cook," for example, as in the derisive "Why, that fellow doesn't amount to Hannah Cook!"—an expression our New England ancestors would have immediately recognized, but which if used today would draw only blank stares. Just who was this unfortunate female, this epitome of worthlessness, whose very name was once synonymous with "good-for-nothing, useless member of the community?" Why, none other than "hand nor cook," that's who. That is to say, the name is a corruption of the phrase, which would have been used of someone who had been tried on board as a *hand* at various levels of skill, and as a last resort, as *cook*, and had proven to be of no value in any of these positions.

I've omitted others because they seem to be too technical while at the same time too obscure. Charles Nordhoff, for example, in his book of memoirs, *Whaling and Fishing* (published in 1856) mentions "the 'ram-cat' (the sailors' name for a cabin stove)." Sources I've consulted cite *ram-cat* as slang for "a man wearing furs," as in "ram-cat cove." Cove, of course, is British slang for "fellow." I suspect the sailors' use of *ram-cat* for "stove" is an instance of Cockney rhyming slang, another example of which is *China* meaning "mate"—a shortening of the term "china plate," which rhymes with mate. I have therefore chosen to exclude *ram-cat* because it is obscure and not strictly speaking a nautical expression.

Purists may argue that I have been inconsistent in my choices. Is **long pig** truly a *nautical* expression? The honest answer is, perhaps not, but it was first heard (and translated from the Fiji) by seamen, and became a term they readily used (sometimes under unfortunate circumstances, i.e., when compelled, out of dire necessity, to themselves partake of this culinary delicacy).

Is **forecastle** an expression, or merely the name of a structure on a ship? Undoubtedly the latter. But the "castle" part of it betrays the antiquity of the word and is representative of the antiquity of sea terms in general—and the rich heritage of our language. During the Middle Ages warships were virtual floating fortresses. Each had two wooden towers or "castles": tall structures from which crude bombs (or fire pots) and boiling oil could be hurled down upon the enemy. Gradually, the aftercastle was eliminated and only the forecastle remained, as quarters for the crew.

Is **admiral of the narrow seas** still commonly used in everyday speech? No, but it once was, and it remains a colorful expression, which is the reason why I've included it.

Just the other day while dining in a restaurant on Cape Cod I came upon the expression **Splice the main brace!** I had thought it obsolete, but there it was, embroidered on an ensign hanging prominently from the ceiling for all to see. The ensign was actually an advertising banner (one of many such "collectibles" used as decorations in The British Beer Company Restaurant and Pub on Route 6A in Sandwich) for Pusser's Rum. "Drink Pusser's! Support the Royal Navy Sailor's Fund." Just how drinking Pusser's (splicing the main brace) would help the sailor's fund wasn't specified, but no doubt there was a connection, and I lifted my **schooner** of Scottish ale in respectful toast.

On a subsequent visit to the restaurant (highly recommended, by the way, for their excellent selection of ales and equally excellent pizzas) I took the time to read an advertisement for Pusser's printed on a stand-up card listing various rum concoctions (including grog). I doubt that the Pusser's people will object if I quote from the "Pusser's Rum Story": "For over 300 years, from 1665 to July 31st, 1970, the jack tars of Great Britain's Royal Navy were issued a daily ration (tot) of Admiralty rum by the Purser, known to the Navy as the 'Pusser.'" (For more on the grog story, see the entry for **groggy**.)

Much of the pleasure derived from putting together this book has been in the pursuit of the origins of the phrases. I've consulted numerous reference books, and wherever possible, have looked to original sources. Even so, the etymologies of many of the terms and expressions have been lost in antiquity, or are the subject of controversy or disagreement amongst experts. **Horse latitudes** is a case in point. Of the two explanations put forth, I favor the one involving the unfortunate disposal of horses at sea. I do so not for scholarly reasons, but simply because friends of mine own an old farm they've humorously dubbed The Horse Latitudes, because of all the elderly and otherwise unwanted horses that over the years have been "dumped" on them.

At the same time, I've scrupulously avoided folk etymologies: incorrect popular notions as to the origin of a word or phrase. For example, some years ago on the island of Nantucket I was told by a tour guide, as we passed an old windmill, that the phrase **three sheets to the wind** (designating a state of inebriation) originated by analogy to a damaged windmill. The four blades of a windmill were typically covered with canvas; if the canvas (or sheet) of one of the blades was torn or tattered, the other three blades would flap wildly out of control. The trouble with this explanation is that it has no basis in fact. The "sheets" referred to are chains or ropes (as evinced by this humorous passage from Joan Druett's *Hen Frigates*: "Fidelia reported enjoying a chuckle of her own, however, when she overheard her husband [the captain] call some common old ropes 'the sheets!'"

Most experts are in agreement that the expression **three sheets to the wind** is nautical in origin.

However, the temptation to speculate is difficult to resist. The etymology of the whalemen's cry, **Old Hallett**, will probably never be known. And yet... Hallett is a venerable Cape Cod name; in researching various subjects I've come across any number of sea captains by that name. More to the point there was, in the eighteenth or nineteenth century, living in a crude hut on the dunes of Provincetown, a notorious witch named Goodie Hallett. Ms. Hallett was known to have two familiars, a black cat and a black goat, both of which on occasion rode on the backs of porpoises. According to folklorist Elizabeth Reynard, whenever seamen from the lower Cape "saw two green eyes staring from the spume, [they] exclaimed: 'Thar be Goodie Hallett's familiar waitin' to pick up souls.'" I believe there could very well be a connection between Goodie Hallett and the whalemen's cry, but I can offer no supporting evidence, and so only mention it here, and not in the book proper.

I've also chosen to omit a number of phrases whose nautical origin, while accepted by some, is questioned by others. For example, several explanations for "over a barrel" (*in a vulnerable position; to be at someone's mercy*) are offered by pundits. Two of these explanations point to the sea. The first, and most prevalent, suggests that the custom of tying a man about to be flogged over the barrel of a deck cannon gave rise to this expression. The second, somewhat less accepted, suggests that victims rescued from drowning were revived, and the water expelled from their lungs, by draping them over a barrel and rolling it back and forth.

But could not the cannon to which the wretch was lashed be at a fort in the middle of the desert? And the near-drowning victim have been rescued from a pond far from any sea? I could list a dozen, even a score, of so-called "nautical" terms whose relationship to the sea is a bastard one, at best. Oh, but why quibble? To quote that most famous of **old salts**, Popeye, "I says what I means and I means what I says!"

For whom is the book intended? Why, ye landlubber! for students, writers, wordsmiths, historians, folklorists and other lovers of language and our cultural heritage, as well as for the idly curious and those for whom a story about the history of words is about as good as it gets.

For sailors have their own names, even for things that are familiar ashore; and if you call a thing by its shore name, you are laughed at for an ignoramus and a landlubber. This first day I speak of, the mate having ordered me to draw some water, I asked him where I was to get the pail; when I thought I had committed some dreadful crime; for he flew into a great passion, and said they never had any pails *at sea, and then I learned that they were always called* buckets.

—*Herman Melville,* Redburn

"A dead whale, or a stove boat.": *the slogan of proud whalemen, memorialized by the statue of a heroic harpooner in front of the public library in New Bedford, Massachusetts.* The pursuit of whales in open boats—which in panic or self-defense the whales often stove in—was an extremely hazardous undertaking. "At sea, the best English they speak, is the South Seaman's slogan in lowering away, 'A dead whale, or a stove boat!' Game to the marrow, these fellows are generally selected for harpooners; a post in which a nervous, timid man would be rather out of his element."—Herman Melville, *Omoo;* "Presently one rose, and spouted a short distance ahead of my boat; I made all speed towards it, came up with, and struck it; feeling the harpoon in him, he threw himself, in agony, over towards the boat…and stove a hole in her."—Owen Chase, *Shipwreck of the Whaleship Essex;* "'And what do ye next, men?' / 'Lower away, and after him!' / 'And what tune is it ye pull to, men?' / 'A dead whale or a stove boat!'"—Herman Melville, *Moby Dick*

Admiral Brown: *(a humorous reference to) human feces floating in the ocean.* A ship becalmed on the seas for a long period of time might find itself surrounded by waste from the "seat of ease."

admiral of the narrow seas: *a man who, when drunk, vomits into the lap of the person sitting next to him.* A confined area might be thought of, metaphorically, as a narrow sea.

albatross around one's neck: *an encumbrance or hindrance (often with the implication of condign punishment).* A common superstition among seamen was that gulls and other oceanic birds were the spirits, or souls, of drowned sailors. The appearance of an albatross at sea was a sign of good fortune, but to kill a gull or other bird, especially an albatross, would bring bad luck. The poet William Wordsworth suggested to his friend Samuel Taylor Coleridge that this superstitious belief might form the basis for an interesting poem. Coleridge liked the idea, and wrote *The Rime of the Ancient Mariner.* "At length did cross an Albatross, / Through the fog it came; / As if it had been a Christian soul." [The mariner kills the albatross with a shot from his crossbow, thereby bringing on bad weather, and the enmity of his fellow sailors.] "Ah! well-a-day! what evil looks / Had I from old and young! / Instead of the cross, the Albatross / About my neck was hung." Unfortunately, this reverence for sea birds was not universal. To amuse themselves, sailors sometimes deliberately caught albatrosses with fish hooks, and found entertainment watching the frantic birds clumsily attempt to attain flight from the deck of the ship. When the fashion for bird feathers as ornaments for ladies' hats was at its height, albatrosses were killed for their feathers. "We [left] the remains of Louie in the keeping of the sea-gulls and three large albatrosses, soaring gracefully in the dull grey sky overhead, with their huge wings spread out as though pronouncing a final benediction on the departed soul. (It is a sailor's superstition that these birds are the reincarnated spirits of departed sea captains lost in the bleak, stormy region of Cape Horn.)"—Frederick Perry, *Fair Winds & Foul*; "...the only way to calm the ire of the air and sea spirits offended by the killing of the bird was to tie its carcass around the killer's neck and lash him to the mainmast without food or drink until the storm was over."—James Clary, *Superstitions of the Sea*

All aboard!: *a call for passengers to get onto a train, bus, or other vehicle or vessel.* Originally, a call for all passengers to get onto the sailing vessel. "Board" is an ancient term for a ship's side (constructed of boards).

all at sea: *confused; perplexed; "without a clue."* The sea is vast; on it one easily becomes lost. "As they were first voyagers, they were literally 'all at sea' for the first few days and for a considerable time thereafter, lacking the advantage of advice from elder boys in the half-deck with them…"—William H.S. Jones, *The Cape Horn Breed*

any port in a storm: *in an emergency anything will do.* This expression calls to mind the old saying, "Beggars can't be choosers."

A-1 (or **A-one**): *excellent; first-class.* The insurers, Lloyd's, employed a system for rating ships. The letter referred to the condition of the hull, the number to the quality of the equipment. A-1 designated the top rating. "'…if any of you chaps are looking to ship on a nice clean A-1 California clipper, now's your chance.'"—Frederick Perry, *Fair Winds & Foul*; "'He must be a first-rater,' said Sam. 'A-1,' replied Mr. Roker."—Charles Dickens, *Pickwick Papers*; "Thousand-tongued Rumor says—'her Captain & officers rank A. No.1, both as gentlemen and Seamen.'"—Enoch Carter Cloud, *Enoch's Voyage: Life on a Whale Ship*; "Whaling-captains came from far to survey it. With one voice they pronounced it 'A1,' and in their opinion 'fit to smash ice.'"—Joshua Slocum, *Sailing Alone Around the World*

as much in the way as a reefer: *(said aboard ship of someone useless).* Reefers are midshipmen. "These boys are sent to sea, for the purpose of making commodores; and in order to become commodores, many of them deem it indispensable forthwith to commence chewing tobacco, drinking brandy and water, and swearing at the sailors. As they are placed on board a sea-going ship to go to school and learn the duty of a Lieutenant; and until qualified to act as such, have few or no special functions to attend to; they are little more, while midshipmen, then supernumeraries on board. Hence, in a crowded frigate, they are so everlastingly crossing the path of both men and officers, that in the navy it has become a proverb, that a useless fellow is *'as much in the way as a reefer.'"*—Herman Melville, *White-Jacket*

at loose ends: *in a state of disorder; without plans or direction.* From a crew's need for neatly coiled ropes, for safety and efficiency's sake. "They purposed making for Newcastle under jury-sails; for their mainsail had been blown to ribbons, even the jigger had been blown away, and her rigging flew at loose ends."—Joshua Slocum, *Sailing Alone Around the World*

at slack water: *at a lull.* The period when the tide (high or low) is not visibly moving is called slack water.

at the helm: *in a position of leadership.* The helm of a ship is the tiller or wheel. "The two men at the helm were lashed to the wheel to prevent them from being washed overboard."—Edward Lacey, quoted in *Diaries from the Days of Sail*; "I was glad to have a sailor of Howard's experience on board to witness her performance of sailing with no living being at the helm."—Joshua Slocum, *Sailing Alone Around the World*; "You can depend upon it, Beresford was at the reins (I was going to say 'at the helm') with the coachman and syce stowed away inside." —W.H. Angel, *The Clipper Ship "Sheila"*

B

back and fill: *to act indecisively; shilly-shally; hem and haw.* To maneuver a vessel in a tight space by alternately filling the sails for forward motion then letting them fall astern. "The captain now gave out his orders rapidly and fiercely, sheeting home the topsails and backing and filling the sails, in hope of starting or clearing the anchors; but it was all in vain…"—Richard Henry Dana, Jr., *Two Years Before the Mast*; "The pilot knew his work, and by backing and filling worked up the nine miles to Pagoda Anchorage…" — Thomas Garry Fraser, *Captain Fraser's Voyages*; "I stood the backing and filling on that schooner for three months and then I left her." —George Fred Tilton, *"Cap'n George Fred" Himself*; "One of the men was selected to make the drawing; for a long time he backed and filled; at length, with a desperate grab, he plucked the short straw, which meant we were to take to the beach." —John Cameron, *John Cameron's Odyssey*

batten down the hatches: *to get ready for a storm (or other adversity).* A hatch is an opening in the deck of a ship leading to the hold. A *hatch* is also the covering for the opening. "To batten down" is to secure the covering with thin strips of wood. "For it we took every possible precaution: battened down the hatches; secured the steam launch in the davits; braced the yards up sharp; overhauled the riding tackle."—John Cameron, *John Cameron's Odyssey*; "After a fortnight's sweating, we had our cargo well stowed and trimmed, and we battened down the hatches."—Sir James Bisset, *Sail Ho!*

beachcomber: *tramp; vagrant; someone who lives off what he or she finds washed up on a beach.* A long cresting wave that rolls onto a beach is a breaker, or comber. (The action of the wave is similar to that of a comb.) "'I'm nothing more nor a bloody *beach-comber*,' retorted Salem, stepping forward piratically and eyeing him. [footnote] This is a term much in vogue among sailors in the Pacific. It is applied to certain roving characters, who, without attaching themselves permanently to any vessel, ship now and then for a short cruise in a whaler; but upon the condition only of being honorably discharged the very next time the anchor takes hold of bottom; no matter where. They are, mostly, a reckless, rollicking set..."—Herman Melville, *Omoo*; "...the gang of beachcombers along the water-front...would find some excuse to break into the fracas and either beat him up or have some greaser stick a knife into him before he got through."—Frederick Perry, *Fair Winds & Foul*; "We left him to become a 'beachcomber,' the meanest and lowest expression that can be found in a sailor's vocabulary."—William Fish Williams, quoted in *One Whaling Family*; "They were of that kind who loaf about saloons until want drives them off on a short voyage—they always desert at the next port. Ashore they are known as bums; at sea as beach-combers." —Albert Sonnichsen, *Deep Sea Vagabonds*

before the mast: *(to serve) as a common sailor.* The quarters for sailors were located forward of the foremast. Hence the title of Richard Henry Dana, Jr.'s classic *Two Years Before the Mast*, his account of a two-year's voyage, begun in 1834, on which he served as a common sailor aboard a brig out of Boston. "There were also a second and third mate, a carpenter, sailmaker, steward, cook, etc., and twelve, including boys, before the mast."—Richard Henry Dana, Jr., *Two Years Before the Mast*; "No, when I go to sea, I go as a simple sailor, right before the mast, plumb down into the forecastle, aloft there to the royal masthead."—Herman Melville, *Moby Dick*

Belay your jaw tackle!: *Shut up!* Although the more common meaning for *belay* is "to secure or make fast," it also means "to stop." *Tackle* is gear, or more precisely, in the nautical sense, a system of ropes and blocks used for raising and lowering. "No sooner were we on board ship than he began to follow me about the deck with the aim of unfolding his story; I begged him, however, to belay his jaw tackle until work was over for the day and I could listen in peace."— John Cameron, *John Cameron's Odyssey*

berth: *a bunk or bed on a railroad car.* Originally, a bunk or other sleeping space on a ship. Another, older nautical meaning is space at a wharf for a ship to dock. By extension, the word came to mean a position of employment on a ship. "At length, as the best of a bad bargain, we selected a berth in eight fathoms amid shoals."—John Cameron, *John Cameron's Odyssey*; "I first got a berth as third officer in the ship *Phoebe Dunbar*." —W.H. Angel, *The Clipper Ship "Sheila"*

bilge: *nonsense; foolish talk.* "Bilge" in this sense is a shortening of "bilgewater." The bilge is the lowest inner part of a ship's hull, where (foul) water collects.

binnacle list: *sick list.* The binnacle was the nonmagnetic stand upon which the compass was mounted. The list of men too sick to report for duty was kept there.

binnacle word: *an affected or too literary word (which the sailors would jeeringly offer to chalk up on the binnacle).* They would write such a word there because, presumably, it was a conspicuous location.

bitter end: *the absolute end; a disastrous finish.* Bitts are stout posts set on the deck of a ship to secure cables. The extreme end of the cable that is fastened to the bitt is called the bitter end. The expression probably originated when the anchor cable, being payed out, came to the bitter end. "As a consequence of this criminal folly the anchor chains were run out to the bitter ends…"—John Cameron, *John Cameron's Odyssey*

blackbirding: *engaging in the slave trade.* An obvious euphemism. "After that she was in some dreadful blackbirding business in a far quarter of the South Pacific." —Frank Norris, "The Ship That Saw a Ghost"; "Traders were not looked upon with a friendly eye as most of them were in reality 'blackbirders'; that is, they were after natives to work the Fiji Island plantations and were not too particular as to how they got them."—William Fish Williams, quoted in *One Whaling Family*; "He decided to have a try at blackbirding, or recruiting labor in the South Seas for Hawaiian sugar plantations." —John Cameron, *John Cameron's Odyssey*

bleed the monkey: *to steal rum from the mess tub.* "Monkey" was slang for the mess tub. To bleed was to take blood from a patient (surgically or with leeches).

blow off steam: *to release pent-up energy or emotion.* From the days of steamships.

blow the grampus: *to throw cold water onto a man who is sleeping while on duty.* A grampus is a marine animal similar to a dolphin. "Blow" in this instance means "to spout water and air," something a sleeping man might do when suddenly doused with cold water. "When I got back to the hall the jug was empty, and Mr. Dark was comforting himself with a pinch of snuff, snorting over it like a perfect grampus."—Wilkie Collins, "A Marriage Tragedy"; "…it was a world of bucko mates who lived by bells and woke men who slept while on duty by dropping buckets of water on them…"— Joan Druett, *"She Was a Sister Sailor"*; "Though this fish [the grampus], whose loud sonorous breathing, or rather blowing, has furnished a proverb to landsmen, is so well known a denizen of the deep, yet is he not popularly classed among whales."—Herman Melville, *Moby Dick*

blubber: *to weep or sob noisily.* From association with whale blubber (oily, bubbly). "A man, whom we supposed a boatswain's mate, from the silver whistle hanging from his neck, came below, driving before him a couple of blubbering boys, and followed by a whole troop of youngsters in tears."—Herman Melville, *Omoo*; "Still Jorgensen clung to me with a grip of death, until with a feeling of disgust I laid down the iron, while he blubbered like a child and his hands remained clasped in supplication."—John Cameron, *John Cameron's Odyssey*

blue water: *the open ocean.* Shallow water is green (or muddy, if near the mouth of a river.) "Thank heaven I am again on blue water!"—Edward Ely, *The Wanderings of Edward Ely*; "The color of the water has been changed since we left the Pacific day before yesterday and although it is fresh and green almost disclosing by its transparency the coral sinks and beds of white sand at the bottom, yet to the sailor's eye nothing is so pleasing as the dark blue of the open ocean."—ibid.; "So we had blue water under our keel. Only after getting a good offing did I breathe freely; only then did I feel safe in reducing sail."—John Cameron, *John Cameron's Odyssey*; "The mariner, when drawing nigh the coasts of foreign lands…never rests till blue water is under him again."—Herman Melville, *Moby Dick*

box the compass: *to go through all phases (of action or belief) only to arrive at the point from which one started.* To name all the points of the compass in proper order from north around to north again is to "box the compass." "'Old Noah was the first sailor. And St. Paul, too, knew how to box the compass, my lad!'"—Herman Melville, *White-Jacket*; "'I took my first lesson in navigation this afternoon, commenced learning to box the compass,' Fidelia wrote on August 18, 1853, five days after departure."—Joan Druett, *Hen Frigates*; "[captain to an inexperienced helmsman:] 'Keep her steady, you scoundrel, you're boxing the compass!'"—Herman Melville, *Redburn*; "I had taken no end of salts, and the captain had 'boxed the compass' with the medical chest, all to no avail."—John Kenlon, *Fourteen Years A Sailor*

brace up!: *an exhortation to call up one's courage or fortitude.* The nautical origin is in the handling of square sails; to "brace up" is to swing the yards into such a position that they will take best advantage of the wind and therefore perform most efficiently. "We have become accustomed to these little 'head winds,' however & have only to 'brace up' and 'beat to windward!'"—Enoch Carter Cloud, *Enoch's Voyage: Life on a Whale Ship*

brass-bounder: *a midshipman or apprentice.* The following gives as complete (albeit biased) an explanation of this term as could be desired: "They are boys whose parents have paid a certain premium that their sons may go to sea with a shabby gentility that keeps them from mixing with common sailors. They are bound as cadets or apprentices for four years, during which time they are supposed to become able seamen...But the truth is, few of them are ever found capable. Most of these boys are the black sheep of well-to-do families, good for nothing ashore, less serviceable at sea. Not half of them ever serve their full term. ...real seamen, both officers and men, have dubbed them 'brass-bounders,' on account of their brass-bound uniforms."—Albert Sonnichsen, *Deep Sea Vagabonds*; "How the eyes of him glinted as he looked about, proud of his brass-bound clothes and badge cap."—David W. Bone, *The Brassbounder*; "'Oh, them brassbounders!' he would say. 'Them ruddy know-alls!'"—ibid.

brig: *a military guardhouse.* "Brig" in the sense of a ship's prison is a shortening of *brigantine*, a type of two-masted sailing ship. The word, deriving from *brigand*, originally meant a pirate ship. "After their examination they were ordered into the 'brig,' a jail-house between two guns on the main-deck, where prisoners are kept."—Herman Melville, *White-Jacket*

bring up all standing: *to shock, as with unexpected news.* To strike, i.e., haul down (the masts or sails) a ship in full career with all sails set is to bring it up all standing. "Besides that we were very much in danger of snapping the other chain short off when the ship brought us all standing to her anchor after a clear drift to 90 fathoms."—Edward Ely, *The Wanderings of Edward Ely*; "'…no ship could stand up and take such a squall as she did with all sails set…If she didn't take aback and go down all standing, where the devil did she go to, sir?'"—Frederick Perry, *Fair Winds & Foul*; "Then he went full speed ahead for all he was worth once more, when he was brought up all standing with a jerk through the weight of the ship, which brought her taffrail down level with the water."—W.H. Angel, *The Clipper Ship "Sheila"*

bully beef (also **bullum**): *boiled salt beef.* This term probably originates from the French *bouilli*, meaning boiled meat, or it may be a corruption of *bull beef.* "…Starbuck gave the natives some *bullum*, a salt beef fancied by whalers. *Bullum* was the dried meat of old Nantucket cows, slaughtered in their extreme age, and salted and dried in the sun, like fish."—Eleanor Early, *An Island Patchwork*

bung up and bilge free: *everything aboard ship in excellent order.* Barrels are properly stored with their bungs (holes) in the up position; the bilge is the lowest (inner) section of a ship's hull. "Our water casks were stored in the main hold. They lay on their sides, closely packed, with bung-holes up and the bungs set loosely in place."—Walter Hammond, *Mutiny on the* Pedro Varela

Bungs: *nickname for a ship's cooper.* The ship's cooper is responsible for making and repairing wooden casks, kegs, and barrels. A bung is the stopper that fits into the bunghole in the keg or barrel through which liquid is poured. "Bung" is also the term used for the hole itself.

bunk: *a narrow bed attached to a wall; a place for sleeping.* A shortened form of "bunker," a bin or tank for fuel storage. "In some of these boxes were large chests, which I at once supposed to belong to the sailors, who must have taken that method of appropriating their 'bunks,' as I afterward found these boxes were called."—

Herman Melville, *Redburn*; "Three nights I swashed in my greasy bunk, like a solitary sardine in a box with the side knocked out."—Charles Warren Stoddard, *South Sea Idyls*

by and large: *for the most part; in any case; generally speaking.* From "taking it by and large"; considering a ship's performance on all points of sailing. ("Large" designates a favorable wind.) "No part of the voyage up to this point, taking it by and large, had been so finished as this."—Joshua Slocum, *Sailing Alone Around the World*; "By and large I have not spent a more pleasurable forty-six days than in Calcutta, notwithstanding the fact that I went to a hospital with dengue fever, a tropical disease that left my joints aching and head bursting with pain."—John Cameron, *John Cameron's Odyssey*

C

caboose: *the last car on a freight train, with cooking facilities and sleeping quarters for the crew.* The small deck-house on a sailing ship where cooking was done; a ship's galley. "…our old cook used to keep himself shut-up in his caboose, a little cook-house, and never told any of his secrets."—Herman Melville, *Redburn*; "Presently some of the seamen emerged on deck, pannikins in hand, and went to the door of the caboose."—Sir James Bisset, *Sail Ho!*; "At this, the seamen told the cook to clear out of his caboose, or he'd be thrown out."—ibid.

Cape Cod turkey: *salted cod fish.* One old recipe, possibly with Thanksgiving Day in mind, includes the instructions, "Stuff and sew up the fish." Also called Block Island turkey. "Our Christmas dinner consisted of plain duff and turkey (Cape Cod) [footnote: Salt fish] which of course brought a big growl from the forecastle…" —Frederick Pease Harlow, *The Making of a Sailor*

cardinal point: *the essentials of a discourse or policy.* North, south, east, and west are the cardinal or principal points of the compass.

careen: *to lurch or swerve while moving rapidly; (slang: to lurch or sway while drunk).* To careen is to roll a ship over (for cleaning or repair) until the keel is exposed. "Careen" derives from *carina*, the Latin word for "keel."

carry away: *to move or greatly excite.* During storms (or dirty weather), masts and other equipment are often carried away by wind or waves. "We shortly after sailed on a cruise in the north seas and encountered a dreadful gale...I never was in such danger in all my life...We in a few hours carried away our bowsprit and foremast in this dreadful night, then our mizen and topmast."—John Nicol, *The Life and Adventures of John Nicol, Mariner*; "In endeavoring to tack, the ship got sternboard and went stern on to a huge lump of ice, splitting the rudder head and carrying away the wheel ropes."—William Reynolds, *Voyage to the Southern Ocean*; "Sliding across the deck and striking the combings of the mizzen hatch, it rolled over and over, bringing up against the spare spars lashed to the bulwarks with such force that had it struck the bulwarks no doubt they would have been carried away and the booby hatch gone overboard. —Frederick Pease Harlow, *The Making of a Sailor*

carry on: *to act in a foolish or inappropriate manner.* From the days of clipper ships; i.e., to carry sails recklessly in order to increase speed. "The captain, however, was anxious to make a record passage; therefore, his officers were obliged to 'carry on.'"—John Kenlon, *Fourteen Years A Sailor*; "A lot depends upon the ability of the ship to carry on sails to the last extremity; and one complaint I had to make against the ship's outfit was that the chain supplied for halyards, ties, and sheets, was not to be depended on."—W.H. Angel, *The Clipper Ship "Sheila"*; "The mate, nervously walking the weather gangway on the poop, stopped occasionally to cast his eye to windward for any indication of an approaching squall and then with head thrown far back on his shoulders, watched the topgallant sail to see how much longer he could carry on before taking it in, as the wind steadily increased."—Frederick Pease Harlow, *The Making of a Sailor*

castaway: *a rejected person; reprobate.* From the term for a shipwrecked person. "In those days there was little guidance apart from the wrecks of ships and crude landmarks erected by castaways."—Henry H. Bootes, *Deep-Sea Bubbles*; "An error of judgment on the captain's part, and we would be cast away on an icebound, inhospitable shore to starve, possibly to be frozen to death."—George H. Grant, *The Half Deck*

catch a crab: *to miss with an oar while pulling*. "There are various ways of *catching a crab*, as, for example, (1) to turn the blade of the oar or 'feather' under water at the end of the stroke and thus be unable to recover; (2) to lose control of the oar at the middle of the stroke by 'digging' too deeply; or (3) to miss the water altogether."— J.S. Farmer and W.E. Henley, *Slang and Its Analogues*; "Bill was not much of an oarsman for we were no sooner clear from the schooner than he 'caught a crab,' i.e., he couldn't keep his oar from the water, and the mate sang out: 'Here! Here!'"—Frederick Pease Harlow, *The Making of a Sailor*; "Pulling the bow oar, I managed to keep in time with Paul Nelson, and to avoid catching crabs..."— William H.S. Jones, *The Cape Horn Breed*

cat's-paw: *a light wind that ruffles the surface of the sea* (as if rippled by a cat's paw). "The captain now abdicated in the pilot's favor, who proved to be a tiger of a fellow, keeping us hard at work, pulling and hauling the braces, and trimming the ship, to catch the least cat's-paw of wind."—Herman Melville, *Redburn*; "Last night was, literally speaking, as light as day, and its tranquillness was only varied by an occasional catspaw which would ripple the water for a few minutes and then die away again as calm as before."— Edward Ely, *The Wanderings of Edward Ely*; "But in the calms we were 'worked to death,' for at every cat's paw (light and changeable puff of wind) the sails must be trimmed, and retrimmed, and trimmed again to catch advantageously the ever-variable direction of the zephyrs."—Hiram P. Bailey, *Shanghaied out of 'Frisco in the 'Nineties*

caulk: *a surreptitious nap, especially when on duty; a dram (of grog or other alcoholic beverage)*. To caulk is to make a ship or boat watertight by packing the seams. A caulk is therefore something (a drink) that keeps out the wet or the damp. And a drink may cause a person to want to sleep. "Thereafter all hands rigged in warmer clothing and no longer caulked the decks at night; that is, selected soft planks for beds and velvety coils of rope for pillows."—John Cameron, *John Cameron's Odyssey*

Chips: *nickname for a ship's carpenter.* This usage dates back to around 1770, and may derive from an old saying, "A carpenter is known by his chips." "He was the ship's carpenter; and for that reason was sometimes known by his nautical cognomen of 'Chips.'"—Herman Melville, *Omoo*; "Meantime, Chips had forgotten his intention of making sausage of the third mate, for he was parading up and down on top of the forward house, brandishing his axe..."—Frederick Perry, *Fair Wind & Foul*; "These South Sea Whales are not remarkable for docility either and I expect that 'old chips' (Carpenter) will have a job of mending boats!"—Enoch Carter Cloud, *Enoch's Voyage: Life on a Whale Ship*; "CHIPS—Sailors' term, for ship's Carpenter. Repairer afloat of all timber and ironwork damage; sounder of the ship's well; locator of leaks. Goes aloft and inspects all ironwork, and working parts; an indispensable man."—Hiram P. Bailey, *Shanghaied out of 'Frisco in the 'Nineties*

chock-a-block: *squeezed together; jammed; drunk or filled to repletion.* When a ship's tackle has been pulled up to its limit, the pulleys (chocks) or blocks are so close together that there is no space between. "By hauling the reef tackles chockablock, we took the strain from the other earings..."—Richard Henry Dana, Jr., *Two Years Before the Mast*; "'If it warn't for having one too many, there wouldn't be any crowding and jamming in the mess. I'm blessed if we aren't about chock a' block here!'"—Herman Melville, *White-Jacket*; "'...for those masts are rooted in a hold that is going to be chock a' block with sperm-oil, d'ye see...'"—Herman Melville, *Moby Dick*; "Oh, those never-to-be-forgotten days, so dear to the heart of a deep-water man, when the lower reaches of the Thames were chock-a-block with famous ships."—Henry H. Bootes, *Deep-Sea Bubbles*

clear out: *to go away (often used in anger or irritation as a command).* From a vessel's being free to depart from a port after obtaining the necessary clearance papers. "The vessel was wrecked, and my shipmates cleared out, leaving me behind."—John Cameron, *John Cameron's Odyssey*; "The usual thing is in such procedure for the tug to assist, by keeping ahead and gradually slacking back, but in this case they let all go on board the tug and cleared out."—W.H. Angel, *The Clipper Ship "Sheila"*; "My father sensed that, if I didn't get the sack, I would resign, sooner or later, and clear out to sea…"—Sir James Bisset, *Sail Ho!*; "'It was either clear out or go stark raving mad, and I preferred the former, so I got out and never wish to land in Patagonia again.'"—Henry H. Bootes, *Deep-Sea Bubbles*

cockpit: *the space in an airliner housing the pilot and crew.* A cockpit is a place where cockfights are held. It became a slang or humorous term for the compartment housing junior officers on a warship, because that is where the wounded were carried during a sea fight. "Some hands were sent down to manage the boat and we were sent down to the cockpit and patched up by the surgeon." —John Wetherell, *The Adventures of John Wetherell*

come in through the hawse-hole: *to enter the service at the lowest grade; to rise in rank from the forecastle.* A hawse-hole is an opening in the bow through which a hawser (rope or cable used in mooring a ship) is passed. "I always remembered, in dealing with my crews, my own yearnings when I formerly occupied their present positions; for I also entered sea life by coming on board through the hawse-pipes."—W.H. Angel, *The Clipper Ship "Sheila"*

come to the end of one's rope: *to run out of options; not know what to do next.* Any number of instances of running out of rope while attempting to work the sails of a ship would have given rise to this expression.

coming down by the run: *headlong descent.* From objects (sails or cargo) being hoisted up then suddenly let drop by running the rope loose.

crow's-nest: *a lookout perch or platform attached to a high structure.* On a whaling ship, the crow's-nest is attached to or near the head of a mast. "We had built the 'crow's-nest' before we reached the Sea, a canvas covered frame placed on the topmast crosstrees of the foremast, and regular masthead watches were stood by the officers and boatsteerers."—William Fish Williams, quoted in *One Whaling Family*; "…it is much to be deplored that the mastheads of a southern whale-ship are unprovided with those enviable little tents or pulpits, called *crow's-nests*, in which the lookouts of a Greenland whaler are protected."—Herman Melville, *Moby Dick*

cut and run: *to depart hastily.* There are two explanations for this expression. In an emergency, there was no time to raise the anchor, so the cable was cut. Or, the ropes attaching the sails to the yards were cut. "We have had several fires here this winter, some of them close to our ship so that we were all ready to 'cut and run' several times." —Edward Ely, *The Wanderings of Edward Ely*; "'I'll have to watch my step when I go up town again, for if this woman ever sets eyes on me I'll have to tack ship in a hurry, for she's got a dirty tongue. If her language tonight is any criterion, believe me I'll cut and run before laying to, to hear what she's got to say.'"—Frederick Pease Harlow, *The Making of a Sailor*

cut of (one's) jib: *appearance, style, or manner.* The jib is a triangular sail stretched from the foretopmast head to the jib boom or bowsprit. "We narrowly watched their rig and the cut of their jibs, and how they walked the water, for there was all the difference between them that there is between living creatures."—Henry David Thoreau, *Cape Cod*

cut the painter: *to decamp, make off suddenly and secretly; to die.* A painter is a rope attached to the bow of a boat for tying up. "'Stand by to cut the painter, Tommy-boy! Stand by the releasing gear, Percy!'"—George H. Grant, *The Half Deck*; "When a sailor died he either 'cut his painter,' 'slipped his cable,' 'went aloft,' or 'unraveled his lifeline.'"—James Clary, *Superstitions of the Sea*;

"'He's coiled his last rope, I guess,' whispered the sailor from Baltimore. 'He'll heave anchor soon.'"—Hiram P. Bailey, *Shanghaied out of 'Frisco in the 'Nineties*

D

Davy Jones's locker: *the final resting place of those who perish at sea (the bottom of the ocean).* Davy Jones is sailor's slang for the devil or spirit of the sea. Jones probably derives from Jonah (Jonah and the Whale); St. David is the patron saint of Wales. The term is believed to be Welsh in origin. Locker in this sense is a trunk for storage. "…our heavy main topgallant yard…with the sail attached broke away from its lashings in the main riggings before it was well secured and went to 'Davy Jones.'" —Edward Ely, *The Wanderings of Edward Ely*; "With all their faults, I have a great love for those old sailors of the long voyage, and I hope their dream of a pleasant resting place after clearing Davy Jones' locker will be found for them."—Thomas Garry Fraser, *Captain Fraser's Voyages*; "'He got so frightened about his plaguy soul, that he shrinked and sheered away from whales, for fear of afterclaps, in case he got stove and went to Davy Jones.'"—Herman Melville, *Moby Dick*

Davy Jones's medicine: *seasickness.* "…after the operation of David Jones's medicine (sea-sickness) I felt my health improved, and by the time we arrived in Surinam, I felt quite well, and I found I was able to give pretty good satisfaction in my line of duty."—Elijah Cobb, *A Cape Cod Skipper*

dead beat: *someone who doesn't pay his debts; a lazy person.* To "beat" is to progress against the wind by tacking. Progressing directly into the wind is accomplished only by a "dead beat." According to nautical experts, it is the most wearisome maneuver in sailing. By transference, a dead beat is someone who has given up the struggle. "It has been nothing but a dead beat to windward and against a strong current and heavy sea."—Edward Ely, *The Wanderings of Edward Ely*; "A lusty, big, and apparently good sailor man holding a V.G. discharge of recent date would present himself, and be engaged and sign on; but on mustering the crew, most likely after the ship had been towed to sea from the dock, the men coming on board too drunk to do it before, a miserable specimen would turn up and answer to the name, that was not the man you engaged, but someone personating him (a boarding-master's dead-beat, as it used to be called)."—W.H. Angel, *The Clipper Ship "Sheila"*; "After this exertion we were nearly dead beat, but excitement kept us going as the steamer, now fully in view, was coming up fast."— Sir James Bisset, *Sail Ho!*

deadeye: *(a slang term for) a marksman; a wooden block containing three holes through which lanyards (small lines) are passed.* The block with three holes in it resembled a skull. "DEADEYES— Stout discs of wood through which holes (generally three) are pierced for the reception of thin ropes called *lanyards*."—Hiram P. Bailey, *Shanghaied out of 'Frisco in the 'Nineties*; "After we finished rattling down we began scraping the dead-eyes and other bright woodwork."—Frederick Pease Harlow, *The Making of a Sailor*

dead reckoning: *calculating by guesswork.* Estimating the position of a ship by calculating (taking into consideration such variable factors as winds, tides, and currents) from the direction and distance run since the last observation was known as "dead reckoning." "Inch by inch, as fast as the gale would permit, we made sail on the ship, for the wind still continued ahead, and we had many days' sailing to get back to the longitude we were in when the storm took us...A light southeaster, to which we could carry a reefed topmast studding sail, did wonders for our dead reckoning."—Richard Henry Dana,

Two Years Before the Mast; "I remember that on one occasion when the ship's chronometers were put out of commission by a heavy sea striking under our counter off Cape Horn, we ran from there by 'dead reckoning' to Cape Clear without sighting a vessel or making a land-fall, and we found upon picking up land that we were only fourteen miles out of our true course."—Frederick Perry, *Fair Winds & Foul*; "We freely admit that we are setting forth on an exploratory voyage, and for a spell will have to sail by dead reckoning." — editorial from first (August, 1954) issue of *Down East, The Magazine of Maine*

derelict: *tramp; social outcast.* A ship abandoned at sea is a derelict. "It is impossible to determine how many of these wrecks, instead of sinking, became floating derelicts and endangered other vessels."—James Clary, *Superstitions of the Sea*; "A crew of runners is one of the most motley collections of human beings imaginable … broken-down mates … boilermakers, beachcombers, and almost anything in the shape of a man, even to former captains who through misfortune, but mostly through drink, had become derelicts along the water-front…"—Frederick Perry, *Fair Winds & Foul*; "As we pulled away from the *British Isles*, we had a general view of her battered condition and forlorn appearance, contrasting so unfavorably with that of other ships in the anchorage that she looked like a derelict…"—William H.S. Jones, *The Cape Horn Breed*

dirty weather: *foul, stormy, rough seas; a typhoon or hurricane.* "Observing the steady fall of the barometer, Captain MacWhirr thought, 'There's some dirty weather knocking about.'…He had had an experience of moderately dirty weather—the term dirty as applied to the weather implying only moderate discomfort to the seaman."—Joseph Conrad, *Typhoon*; "We had dirty weather off the Columbia River bar which retained several days."—Thomas Garry Fraser, *Captain Fraser's Voyages*; "We sailed for Greenland, and cruised up off Cape Farewell. There wasn't any ice but the weather was the dirtiest I had ever seen."—George Fred Tilton, *"Cap'n George Fred" Himself*

Do you hear the news?: *Wake up; turn out.* This formulaic expression was used in turning out the relief watch.

Doctor: *nickname for the ship's cook.* "The cook of the vessel is dubbed 'Doctor,' but whether the name was given him on account of his mixing qualities, in concocting palatable dishes for the crew from the salt beef and briny pork with wormy sea biscuits, or in rationing out lime juice, in the hot climates, as a preventive of yellow fever, I am unable to say."—Frederick Pease Harlow, *The Making of a Sailor*; "The cook was a Cockney of a surly temper, who, in accordance with custom, was known as 'the Doctor.'"—Sir James Bisset, *Sail Ho!*; "The ship's cook, known in sailing-ship parlance as the 'Doctor,' had the task of dispatching the hogs to their doom, an operation performed by him with a long knife..."—William H.S. Jones, *The Cape Horn Breed*

dogwatch: *a short watch, two hours instead of the usual four, either from four to six p.m., or from six to eight p.m.* How these two short watches came to be called dogwatch is anyone's guess. "The watches are four hours on deck, and four hours off, until 4 p.m., when there is a so-called dog-watch of two hours until 6 p.m. and another from 6 to 8 p.m.; this is done to alter the time of the watches, as otherwise the crew would be on watch always at the same hours."—W.H. Angel, *The Clipper Ship "Sheila"*; "...the watches were four hours long beginning with the sea day at midnight. While one watch is on deck the other watch is below, except from four to eight in the afternoon and evening which was known as the 'dogwatch,' when all hands were on deck. This...changed the order of the watches."—William Fish Williams, quoted in *One Whaling Family*; "Most pleasant of all was the six to eight dogwatch. It was then that the two sides of the forecastle came together and sang songs or told stories. The watch that went below at four would have tea at five and relieve again at six. The other watch would then have tea and come below."—Albert Sonnichsen, *Deep Sea Vagabonds*; "He was only a second voyager, a dog-watch at sea—almost a greenhorn."—David W. Bone, *The Brassbounder*

donkey's breakfast: *straw mattress*. Donkeys eat straw. "...donkey's breakfast, the cornhusk or straw mattress of the forecastle."—Donald Weston Hall, *Arctic Rovings*; "The tug was loaded to the gunwales with our crew and their dunnage, which consisted of straw beds (familiarly known as 'donkey breakfasts'), sea chests and kit-bags."—Frederick Perry, *Fair Winds & Foul*; "These orders were presented...by a boardinghouse keeper...who...was supposed to provide him with an outfit, including a chest and a mattress, always referred to as a 'donkey's breakfast.'"—William Fish Williams, quoted in *One Whaling Family*; "My equipment was simplicity itself: a mattress of donkey's breakfast, technically known as straw; blankets and pillows; a suit of oilskins; a tin plate; a pot; a pannikin; soap, needles, and thread; and a sheath knife."—John Cameron, *John Cameron's Odyssey*; "I should explain that a 'donkey's breakfast' is a sailor's bed or mattress. It is generally made of some tenth-rate jute sacking about 6 feet long by 2 feet wide, into which straw or hay is stuffed."—Henry H. Bootes, *Deep-Sea Bubbles*

Down East: *Maine (or more generally, New England)*. Because the area's prevailing winds are southwest, ships heading toward Maine from the west and south sail before the wind, i.e., they "run *down*hill," as opposed to "beating up against it," which is what ships going to windward are said to do. "When *Down East* was founded...the name was commonly understood to be synonymous with the state of Maine. The term...has its origins in the days of sail when ships, leaving Boston, sailed downwind to ports along the Maine coast and beyond. They sailed down wind to the east; hence the term *down east*...Where once *Down East* stood for the Maine coast in its entirety from Kittery to Eastport...more and more the term seems reserved for the area east of Ellsworth."—*Down East, The Magazine of Maine*

Down the hatch!: *Drink up!* This toast has its origins in cargoes being lowered into the holds of ships through openings in the deck called hatches; it could also refer to the way seas might pour into the hatches of a foundering vessel. "The opening was surrounded by a combing eighteen inches high to prevent any water shipped in rough weather from pouring down the hatch."—Walter Hammond, *Mutiny on the* Pedro Varela; "The doors of the hurricane house had been lashed to prevent water from coming down the hatchway." —John T. Perkins, quoted in *"She Was a Sister Sailor"* by Joan Druett; "'See that white shark!' cried a horrified voice from the taffrail; 'he'll have that man down his hatchway!'"—Herman Melville, *White-Jacket*; "'Don't sip it,' they advised me. 'Put it down the hatch at one go...'"—Sir James Bisset, *Sail Ho!*

dunnage: *baggage; small personal belongings*. A layer of loose materials (straw, twigs, mats, netting, ropes, and the like) spread on the floor of a ship's hold to protect the cargo. The application of the term to personal belongings was originally facetious. "The ship being now ready, we covered the bottom of the hold over, fore and aft, with dried brush for dunnage, and having leveled everything away, we were ready to take in our cargo."—Richard Henry Dana, Jr., *Two Years Before the Mast*; "And now the search of the sailors' dunnage was completed. All whisky, firearms, stilettos and blackjacks had been confiscated and locked in a place of safety."—Frederick Perry, *Fair Winds & Foul*; "We got wood enough for the galley and for dunnage; that is, to stow between the casks in the hold to prevent them from shifting."—William Fish Williams, quoted in *One Whaling Family*; "So we got our pay and discharges, and, shouldering our dunnage, we went down to the railway station."—Albert Sonnichsen, *Deep Sea Vagabonds*

fagged out: *tired; exhausted.* Strands of badly worn ropes would unravel at the ends; perhaps there is an association with "bedraggled." "Thus it went for three days, until I was fagged out, saw no prospect of better weather, and feared for my health if I had to sit at the tiller without relief..."—John Cameron, *John Cameron's Odyssey*

fathom: *to understand; penetrate the meaning of.* A fathom is a nautical unit equal to six feet. To "fathom" is to determine the depth of. By extension, to fathom is "to get to the bottom of." Fathom derives from an Old English word meaning to embrace (hence the measurement of six feet—the full stretch of both arms).

Fiddler's Green: *the sailors' heaven.* A place of wine, women, music, and merriment. "'Vere *ees* Feedlers Green, Cheeps?'... 'Why, you darned old square-head, think yew hev mast-headed me, eh?...Wall, then, its exact nautical position is as near as dammit ten miles sou-sou-west of 'ell.'"—Hiram P. Bailey, *Shanghaied out of 'Frisco in the 'Nineties*; "I should like to see the doctor's eyes twinkle and once again hear his peaty Irish brogue. Who says I shall not? Perhaps there truly is a place called Fiddler's Green."—John Cameron, *John Cameron's Odyssey*

figurehead: *someone apparently in charge, but with no actual*

authority. From the carved ornamental figure placed on the prow of a ship, a practice dating back to pagan times. In fact, the first figures were not ornamental but (in a sense) practical. Each figurehead represented the goddess to whom the ship was dedicated. Her function—at the prow—was to help find the way. "…the eyes were carefully done in order that, though the watch dozed forward, the vessel could pick her own way through danger and destruction."—Horace P. Beck, *The Folklore of Maine*; "As for steering, they never would let me go to the helm, except during a calm, when I and the figure-head on the bow were about equally employed."—Herman Melville, *Redburn*; "Our figure-head suggested (woodenly) a neat, but somewhat rotund lady, perhaps a goddess, painted snow white, with strangely staring blue eyes."—Hiram P. Bailey, *Shanghaied out of 'Frisco in the 'Nineties*

filibuster: *to use delaying tactics (such as prolonged speeches on the Senate floor)*. An older meaning of filibuster is "to engage in a private military action in a foreign country." The word derives from a Dutch word meaning *pirate*. It earned its present meaning when a senator accused an opponent, metaphorically, of "filibustering against the United States." "…the *Glarus*…had first lost her reputation, seduced into a filibustering escapade down the South American coast…"—Frank Norris, "The Ship That Saw a Ghost"; "He was a filibuster in Central America and Cuba, and engaged in gun-running."—Thomas Garry Fraser, *Captain Fraser's Voyages*

first-rate: *foremost in quality or rank*. From the classification of the five sizes, or rates, of British ships of war. The rating was based on the number of guns the ship carried. A ship of one hundred or more guns was first-rate (and would have eight hundred men aboard). "The *Britannia* is a first-rate, carrying 110 guns…She was the strongest built ship in the navy."—John Nicol, *The Life and Adventures of John Nicol, Mariner*

fishing expedition: *a search for evidence of wrongdoing without any preconceived notion other than a hunch*. The literal expression dates back to the days when European vessels went on long voyages to the coast of the New World in search of fish.

flogging (or **whipping**) **through the fleet**: *being flogged on first one's own ship, then on all the others in the fleet. (Sometimes the flogging took place on a large boat that was rowed through the fleet, stopping at each ship so that all could view the punishment.)* This severe form of punishment was often fatal. "…there still remains another practice which, if anything, is even worse than keel-hauling. This remnant of the Middle Ages is known in the Navy as 'flogging through the fleet.'"—Herman Melville, *White-Jacket*; "One of our men was whipped through the fleet for stealing some dollars from a merchant ship…It was a dreadful sight: the unfortunate sufferer tied down on the boat and rowed from ship to ship, getting an equal number of lashes at the side of each vessel from a fresh man."—John Nicol, *The Life and Adventures of John Nicol, Mariner*

flotsam: *wreckage that floats after a ship has sunk; (by extension) drifters, vagrants.* Often seen in the phrase, "flotsam and jetsam." "There were also whites of many nationalities, the human flotsam and jetsam known as 'beachcombers,' who were stranded in all these West Coast ports, living on their wits, or by taking odd jobs, to earn enough money for a perpetual spree on *pisco* and other cheap wines and spirits…"—William H.S. Jones, *The Cape Horn Breed*

forecastle: *short raised deck on the bow; the structure on the upper deck of a ship toward the bow; on a merchant ship, the superstructure housing the crew.* The word is also spelled **fo'c's'le**, which is representative of its pronunciation. (Originally, it was a castle-like structure whose purpose was to overlook the enemy's decks.) "Most persons know that a ship's forecastle embraces the forward part of the deck about the bowsprit: the same term, however, is generally bestowed upon the sailor's sleeping-quarters, which occupy a space immediately beneath, and are partitioned off by a bulkhead."—Herman Melville, *Omoo*; "No man can be a sailor, or know what sailors are, unless he has lived in the forecastle with them." —Richard Henry Dana, Jr., *Two Years Before the Mast*; "The forecastles of most of our ships are small, black, and wet holes, which few landsmen would believe held a crew of ten or twelve men on a voyage of months or years."—ibid.

forge ahead: *to move forward forcefully*. From the forward momentum aided by a ship's weight. "While Degreaves hurried to call Captain Tripp, I took in all sail and dropped both anchors to prevent the brig forging ahead. She came to a dead stop." —John Cameron, *John Cameron's Odyssey*

full and by: *sailing with the yards braced up and the sails full; sailing with the wind ahead of the beam (against the wind)*. "...for we were now sailing 'full and by,' which in the case of our ship meant sailing within six points. That is, we were sailing W.N.W. to the wind due north—our set course."—Hiram P. Bailey, *Shanghaied out of 'Frisco in the 'Nineties*; "'Full an' by,' was the word. 'Full an' by,' an' no damned shinnanikin!"—David W. Bone, *The Brassbounder*; "At two bells (9 A.M.) we set the flying-jib with orders to keep her 'full and by' (as near the wind as she would hold without the sails flapping)."—Frederick Pease Harlow, *The Making of a Sailor*; "Taking a chair next to me, she looked me 'full and by' in the face, for I was a bashful lad..."—ibid.

full speed ahead: *to proceed at the maximum rate*. From the days of steamships.

G

gam: *to gather socially; visit (especially at sea)*. A "gam" is a pod of whales. Herman Melville (in *Moby Dick*) offers this definition: "GAM. Noun—*A social meeting of two (or more) Whale-ships, generally on a cruising-ground; when, after exchanging hails, they exchange visits by boats' crews; the two captains remaining, for the time, on board of one ship, and the two chief mates on the other.*" "He was gamming, the practice of visiting at sea. Captains got together on one ship, and their first mates on the other, exchanging letters, gossip, and reading material."—Daniel Weston Hall, *Arctic Rovings*; "For the Captain's wife there was a special *gam chair*, so that she could be hoisted aboard, hoops and all, with her petticoats tucked modestly about her."—Eleanor Early, *An Island Patchwork*; "You see a 'gam' meant much to me, for one thing it brought a good dinner, whether I stayed at home or went aboard the other ship, as the best the ships offered was always brought out on these occasions."—William Fish Williams, quoted in *One Whaling Family*

get a line on: *to obtain information about*. Metaphorically, from making fast to a whale with a harpoon attached to a line, so that it can be followed and killed.

get the drift of: *to understand the meaning of (a statement, narrative, etc.)*. The tide or current (drift) of an area could affect the reckoning of a ship's position. To get the drift would be to understand the direction and force of the current or tide.

get under way: *to make progress.* Probably from the sense of "way" meaning "course."

give a clean bill of health: *to give approval to after a careful investigation.* From the need of a ship and its crew and cargo to be examined by health or other officials before entering a port. "If there were any sick men, or the vessel had come from a port where there was known to have been an outbreak of fever, he put the ship in quarantine...If everything looked good, he issued a clean bill of health."—Joan Druett, *Hen Frigates*; "The brig having a clean bill of health, the doctor's visit was soon over, and the ship-chandler's boat pulled alongside."—John D. Whidden, *Ocean Life in the Old Sailing Ship Days*

give a wide berth: *to keep a distance from; avoid.* An early meaning of "berth" was "sea room" (sufficient space for a ship to maneuver). "...his associating with such a man as Kelly was sufficient cause to give them both a wide berth if he wished to avoid trouble."—Frederick Perry, *Fair Winds & Foul*; "A dangerous place! The best way to avoid accident is to give it a 'wide berth.'"—Enoch Carter Cloud, *Enoch's Voyage: Life on a Whale Ship*; "The Yankee was making shocking bad steering of it, a fine looking wooden ship, with her white cotton sails, but we gave her a wide berth."—W.H. Angel, *The Clipper Ship "Sheila"*; "Then, with this wind on the port quarter, they ran to the southward, giving the Cape Verde Islands a wide berth."—Sir James Bisset, *Sail Ho!*

give some leeway: *allow for some freedom of movement.* The lee is the side of the ship away from the direction from which the wind is blowing. A ship with insufficient leeway is in danger of being driven onto the shore. "The sport—if it could be called such, since no skill was required—was a diversion for us boys, and the subsequent gluttony even more so, as on returning to the ship we could feed on fish till we were sated, like the sea-lions, and could make up some of the leeway in our nutriment…"—William H.S. Jones, *The Cape Horn Breed*

go astern: *to move to the rear; to go backward.* The stern is the rear part of a ship. "No man living ever tried harder to get on than I have and I have been going astern ever since but I shall never give up as long as I have strength."—Charles Pierce, quoted in *Whaling Letters*

go overboard: *to show excessive enthusiasm.* A person on board a ship, if over excited—or working furiously and throwing caution to the winds—might accidentally go overboard (over the side). Likewise, during severe storms objects and equipment were often swept overboard. "Sliding across the deck and striking the combings of the mizzen hatch, it rolled over and over, bringing up against the spare spars lashed to the bulwarks with such force that had it struck the bulwarks no doubt they would have been carried away and the booby hatch gone overboard."—Frederick Pease Harlow, *The Making of a Sailor*

gone by the board: *gone; lost; wrecked; ruined.* "To go by the board" is to be swept overboard ("board" meaning ship's side). "Her rattling shrouds, all sheathed in ice, / With the masts went by the board."— Henry Wadsworth Longfellow, *The Wreck of the Hesperus*; "For though their progenitors, the builders of Babel, must doubtless, by their tower, have intended to rear the loftiest masthead in all Asia, or Africa either; yet…as that great stone mast of theirs may be said to have gone by the board, in the dread gale of God's wrath…" — Herman Melville, *Moby Dick*

grapple with: *to try to understand; attempt to cope.* A grapple (also grapnel) is a hook or anchor used for the purpose of grasping and holding an enemy ship so that it can be boarded.

graybeard: *the name given to the huge breaking waves common off*

of Cape Horn. From the resemblance of its crest to a beard. "We could see the great seas, white-streaked by lash of driven spray, running up into the lowering sky. When day came, and the heaving, wind-swept face of the waters became plain to us, we saw the stormy path round the Horn in its wildest, grandest mood. Stretching far to the black murky curtain—the rear of the last shrieking rain squall—the great Cape Horn greybeards swept on with terrific force and grandeur, their mile-long crests hurtling skywards in blinding foam."—David W. Bone, *The Brassbounder*; "He and the Mate and I sprang into the mizzen rigging as a gigantic graybeard purler crashed from astern onto the poop."—Sir James Bisset, *Sail Ho!*; "The Greybeards of Cape Horn are laughing uproariously at us, in derision, because with our puny strength we have dared to challenge their supremacy and invade their solitudes." —William H. S. Jones, *The Cape Horn Breed*

greasy: (1) *lucky.* This is a whaleman's term, referring to the whale's valuable oil. A greasy captain is one whose voyages prove profitable; a greasy voyage is lucky, or profitable; a greasy ship is a lucky ship. "Selecting good masters, mates and boatsteerers was of obvious importance if you hoped for a 'greasy' voyage."—Everett S. Allen, *Children of the Light*; "And if a ship happened by, while the whale was being sick, it was *greasy luck.*"—Eleanor Early, *An Island Patchwork*; "I salute him with a salutation so familiar in the old days of whaling—'A Greasy Voyage!'"—M.D.C. Crawford, Introduction to *"Cap'n George Fred" Himself* by George Fred Tilton

greasy: (2) *stormy.* (See the entry for "dirty weather.")

groggy: *unsteady on one's legs; shaky.* Grog is rum diluted with water. It was traditionally given to sailors in the British Navy. The term derives from grogram, a coarse fabric of silk, mohair and wool, often stiffened by gum. It was Admiral Edward Vernon who, in 1740, ordered that diluted rum (rather than the full strength they had formerly received) be regularly issued to British sailors. Admiral Vernon customarily wore a cloak made of grogram and was referred to (behind his back!) as Old Grog by the sailors, with whom he was not popular. (Mount Vernon, in Virginia, was named after the Admiral by Lawrence Washington, who served under him.) "While we lay in Leith Roads, a mutiny broke out...The cause was, their captain gave them five-water grog; now the common thing is three-waters. The weather was cold. The spirit thus reduced was, as the mutineers called it, as thin as muslin and quite unfit to keep out the cold."—John Nicol, *The Life and Adventures of John Nicol, Mariner*

H

hail from: *to come from (a place).* Ships passing at sea would hail one another, identifying their ports of origin. "…mostly schooners…engaged in the Grand Banks fisheries, of which at this time there was a fleet of nearly a hundred sail, all hailing from and owned in Marblehead." —John Wetherell, *The Adventures of John Wetherell*

half seas over: *drunk; intoxicated.* Halfway over the sea, i.e., halfway between sobriety and drunkenness. (Or "seas" may refer to waves, the reference being to a seaman staggering on the deck of a ship as it is swept by high seas.) "Half seas over, their kind friends having supplied them with more food and rum, the prisoners were in royal good humor."—John Cameron, *John Cameron's Odyssey*; "Cold and hungry, I reached the Liverpool Sailors' Home in time for a Christmas celebration, attended by every sailor and his girl, all half seas over and having a devil of a time."—ibid.; "A rope net is hung under the gangplank, and one over the side, amidships, to catch anything slipping from the slings in unloading. Poor Jack is often saved a wetting from this precaution, should he fall when coming aboard 'half seas over.'"—Frederick Pease Harlow, *The Making of a Sailor*; "'Drinking hot rum toddies with me every night, till he couldn't see to put on the bandages; and sending me to bed, half seas over, about three o'clock in the morning.'"—Herman Melville, *Moby Dick*

hand, reef, and steer: *to perform the three types of skills required of a sailor.* The three skills are explained in the following: "An A.B. was expected to be proficient in steering a compass course, making a wide variety of knots and splices, and going aloft in rough weather to take in and furl sails—to 'hand, reef & steer,' as it was put."—Julianna FreeHand, *A Seafaring Legacy*; "An ordinary [seaman] must be able to 'hand, reef and steer,' to box the compass, to be acquainted with the running and standing rigging of a ship, to be able to reeve studding sail gear, to loosen and furl light sails, and even perhaps to send down a royal yard."—John Kenlon, *Fourteen Years A Sailor*; "Perhaps it was brutal but they were far better men when the ship returned to San Francisco than when they sailed. They could 'hand, reef and steer'…"—William Fish Williams, quoted in *One Whaling Family*; "'I shipped as ordinary seaman,' said I, 'and an ordinary seaman is supposed to reef, hand and steer.'"—Frederick Pease Harlow, *The Making of a Sailor*

hard and fast: *unyielding; fixed and invariable.* A ship that is secure in port or—the more likely origin of the expression—stranded on a sandbar at high tide!—is said to be hard and fast. "Reaching the *Minnesota*, hard and fast aground, near midnight, we anchored…"—Samuel Dana Greene, *Battles and Leaders of the Civil War*; "In a word, at daybreak on the morning of December 11 the *Spray* ran hard and fast on the beach."—Joshua Slocum, *Sailing Alone Around the World*; "I…gave it no more thought, being busy with the work, until suddenly the ship struck, bringing up on a sand bar with a force that drove her well on, where she lay, heeled over, hard and fast."—John Wetherell, *The Adventures of John Wetherell*

hard pull: *a struggle, as against illness or financial difficulty.* Sailors did not row; rather they pulled (the oar). "Toward evening the wind moderated sufficiently for us to launch our boats with the assistance of the natives. A hard pull brought us to the *Pomare*."—John Cameron, *John Cameron's Odyssey*; "A good place to 'cure' all such foolish notions in the mind of young mad-caps who imagine they have a 'hard pull' in the voyage of life, is a berth on a Whale

Ship!"—Enoch Carter Cloud, *Enoch's Voyage: Life on a Whale Ship*; "It was a hard pull and no sooner did we pick up the slack of the towrope than Bill threw up, in a fit of seasickness, and vomited all over the boat." —Frederick Pease Harlow, *The Making of a Sailor*

hardtack: *a sea biscuit or bread made with flour and water.* "Tack" is an archaic word for food. "Our breakfast was of fried fish, boiled eggs, 'hard tack,' as the sailors term crackers and biscuit, in distinction from loaf bread, which they call 'soft tack'—and coffee, which we drank from large yellow mugs."—Robert Carter, *A Summer Cruise on the Coast of New England*; "Instead of letting the sailors file their teeth against the rim of a hard sea-biscuit, they baked their bread daily in pitiful little rolls."—Herman Melville, *Omoo*; "He declared that my bread, which was ordinary sea-biscuits and easily broken, was not nutritious as his, which was so hard that I could break it only with a stout blow from a maul."—Joshua Slocum, *Sailing Alone Around the World*

hard up: *poor; destitute.* When the tiller has been thrown by the helmsman as far to one side as it will go, it is said to be "hard up," and there is nothing further to be done. (The opposite, "hard down," though heard frequently enough, somehow never came into common use outside of the nautical world. See the last example below.) "The helm was hard up, the after yards shaking, and the ship in the act of wearing."—Richard Henry Dana, Jr., *Two Years Before the Mast*; "I bawled out to the helmsman, 'Hard up!' but she had not fallen off more than a point, before we took the second shock."—Owen Chase, *Shipwreck of the Whaleship Essex*; "However, just as they were in the act of boarding, Captain Drinkwater suddenly put his helm hard up and gibed over his mainsail so that his heavy main boom, driven by a strong breeze, struck his enemy's masts and left her a wreck."—Julianna FreeHand, *A Seafaring Legacy*; "That night she sat alone and wakeful in the stateroom, listening to the roar of the sea, and heard a sudden cry of, 'Breakers ahead! Hard down the helm!' from the deck."—Joan Druett, *Hen Frigates*

have a bone in her teeth (or **mouth**): *move along rapidly (said of sailing vessels)*. The "bone" is the white foam that forms at the bow as the vessel courses along. "… the *Spray*, under reefs, sometimes one, sometimes two, flew before a gale for a great many days, with a bone in her mouth, toward the Marquesas, in the west, which she made on the forty-third day out, and still kept on sailing."—Joshua Slocum, *Sailing Alone Around the World*; "Soon we saw the *Active* smoking up and coming towards us with 'a bone in her mouth.'"—David W. Bone, *The Brassbounder*; "…the ship was listing over under full sail on her south-westerly course, with a freshening wind and 'a bone in her teeth.'" —William H. S. Jones, *The Cape Horn Breed*

head: *latrine*. Originally, a man-of-war's privy. "A short passage off this stateroom led to the captain's 'head' or water closet, which usually had a washstand and locker."—Joan Druett, *"She Was a Sister Sailor"*; "They therefore fall in for all the dirty work, such as greasing down masts, painting yards and stays, and cleaning the heads."—William H. S. Jones, *The Cape Horn Breed*

heave into sight (or **view**): *to come into view.* On the seas, a ship may heave (rise) into view at the crest of a wave. "A herd of bullocks hove in view; I shut my eyes as the horse, an old pacer from the race tracks of the States, flew on at fifty knots."—John Cameron, *John Cameron's Odyssey*; "Shore folk can have but a hazy idea of all that it means to the deep-water sailor when at last, after long voyaging, the port of his destination heaves in sight."—David W. Bone, *The Brassbounder*; "The next Saturday night we all went ashore as usual and the Mission runner soon hove in sight and invited us to attend another entertainment."—Frederick Pease Harlow, *The Making of a Sailor*

hell to pay: *trouble to face.* Possibly from caulking the "hell" planks (those planks on a ship that are difficult to reach).

hen frigate: *a ship on which a captain was accompanied by his wife.*

The captain's children were often included as well. "Vessels carrying the captain's family were sometimes dubbed 'hen frigates'—particularly if the wife was a 'take-charge' type." —Julianna FreeHand, *A Seafaring Legacy*; "*...hen frigate*, the latter a sea phrase, originally applied to a ship, the captain of which had his wife on board, supposed to command him."—*Dictionary of the Vulgar Tongue* (1811)

high and dry: *destitute; powerless*. As the tide recedes, a ship may be left high and dry, and unable to move. "The position of my vessel, now high and dry, gave me anxiety."—Joshua Slocum, *Sailing Alone Around the World*; "All went well until we entered the narrows, when a north-westerly gale drove us high and dry on the beach at Point Turner on the mainland side."—Henry H. Bootes, *Deep-Sea Bubbles*

high line: *a good catch*. The term originated with the Grand Banks fishery. "Some of his men were not to be beaten; several had at different times been "high line" from Harwich; and all were good fishermen."—Charles Nordhoff, *Whaling and Fishing*

hit a snag: *to encounter an unforeseen difficulty*. Snags are trees or parts of trees that are wholly or partially submerged. Hitting one is a hazard faced not only by riverboat captains, but sea captains as well, along the coast or near the mouths of rivers. "We passed many floating tree-trunks and branches in the river. The snows had come away from the Sierra, and there was a spate on Sacramento. We rode over one of the 'snags' with a shudder..."—David W. Bone, *The Brassbounder*

holystone: *sandstone (used for scouring decks)*. Because the stones were used while the sailors where kneeling as if in prayer, they were jocularly called 'holy.' "The holystone is a large, soft stone smooth on the bottom, with long ropes attached to each end, by which the crew keep it sliding fore and aft over the wet, sanded decks. Smaller hand stones, which the sailors call 'prayer books,' are used to scrub in among the crevices and narrow places where the large holystone will not go."—Richard Henry Dana, *Two Years Before the Mast*; "Near him, upon his knees, and in his hand a 'prayer-book' (lump of holystone), knelt the sailor from Baltimore, holystoning, without any marked emotional ecstasy, the poop."— Hiram P. Bailey, *Shanghaied out of 'Frisco in the 'Nineties*; "They all slept in bunks raised eighteen inches above the deck, and twice a day all the decks were holystoned with 'prayer books' and fine sand."—W.H. Angel, *The Clipper Ship "Sheila"*

horse latitudes: *an area in the Atlantic lying north of the trade winds and noted for high barometric pressure and light, variable winds.* One explanation for the term derives from the fact that in the eighteenth century sailing ships were often becalmed in these waters. The livestock, including horses, which they carried would perish and be cast overboard, so that the surface of the sea became littered with their dead bodies. A second explanation is less morbid. It holds that the origin of the expression is the Spanish *golfo de las yeguas*, "the gulf of mares," the area between Spain and the Canary Islands. "In the Horse Latitudes, that is from 28° to 33° north, we fell in with a Spanish barque from Cuba with refugees, bound to Cadiz."—Thomas Garry Fraser, *Captain Fraser's Voyages*; "The *Spray* was booming joyously along for home now, making her usual good time, when of a sudden she struck the horse latitudes, and her sail flapped limp in a calm."—Joshua Slocum, *Sailing Alone Around the World*; "In these 'horse latitudes' the rain comes and goes in streaks like the wind."—Frederick Pease Harlow, *The Making of a Sailor*

hoveller: *a beach-thief; a lawless boatman.* Such a person often lived in a *hovel* (a low, open shed, or other primitive dwelling).

howling fifties: *the degrees of South Latitude between 50 degrees and 60 degrees, a region of strong westerly winds and gales.* For comparison, see the "roaring forties." "During the next few days, we left the Howling Fifties behind us, and passed into the Roaring

Forties, in weather alternating between gale force and strong winds from the westward, but gradually moderating as we approached the coast."—William H. S. Jones, *The Cape Horn Breed*

in a trice: *in a very short period of time.* To trice up is to hoist a sail or other object and secure it, something an experienced sailor could do very quickly. "In a trice one watch raced aloft to furl sail and the other watch ran forward to the forecastlehead with the Mate to make the tug fast."—Sir James Bisset, *Sail Ho!*

in deep water: *in a difficult situation.* Although deep water may not be detrimental to a large ship, it can pose obvious dangers for a small boat—or a swimmer who has strayed far from shore.

in-fit: *shore clothes.* The opposite of outfit. "So I was taken up to Richardson's and there fitted out with an 'in-fit,' which means a suit of shore clothes." —George Fred Tilton, *"Cap'n George Fred" Himself*

in stays: *in the process of coming about.* A stay is a heavy rope or wire cable used to brace a mast or spar.

in the doldrums: *feeling depressed.* The doldrums are areas in the ocean near the equator where the winds are often too light for a ship to make headway. "After ten days of the Doldrums we got a light air from the SSE which gradually freshened to the southeast trade wind."—Thomas Garry Fraser, *Captain Fraser's Voyages*; "The slight veering of the trade winds each day warned us that we were approaching their most southerly limit, and we began to prepare for our hot, disagreeable and irritating thrash through the doldrums, as we were now in about nine degrees north latitude, and longitude thirty degrees west."—Frederick Perry, *Fair Winds & Foul*; "…this was ominous of doldrums. On the 16th the *Spray* entered this gloomy region, to battle with squalls and to be harassed by fitful calms; for this is the state of the elements between the northeast and the southeast trades, where each wind, struggling in turn for mastery, expends its force whirling about in all directions."—Joshua Slocum, *Sailing Alone Around the World*

in the long run: *eventually; after considerable experience.* The long voyage across the ocean, when a vessel and her crew's true qualities are tested (in contrast to short runs from port to port along the coast).

in the offing: *the near future.* The offing is that part of the sea which, though distant, is visible from the shore. "We gradually gained an offing with much trying work for all hands, and cleared the land on the third day from casting off the tug."—Thomas Garry Fraser, *Captain Fraser's Voyages*; "'If we could have kept the head of the mainmast an hour longer, we might have got an offing, and fetched to windward of the shoals; but as it is, sir, mortal man can't drive a craft to windward…'"—James Fenimore Cooper, *The Pilot*; "It was during our visits to the *Morning Star* that I first became aware of danger in the offing."—Walter Hammond, *Mutiny on the* Pedro Varela; "For the rest of the day I had to stay in the offing, at his beck and call."—Sir James Bisset, *Sail Ho!*

in the same boat: *in the same situation.* A boat is a small thing compared to the vast ocean. People "in the same boat" generally share the same risks and responsibilities.

ironclad: *rigid; inflexible; unyielding.* From warships, such as "Old Ironsides" (The U.S.S. Constitution), that were ironclad, that is, sheathed in iron plates. "Whoever bought the parcel had to tear down the existing house and rebuild away from the water. That was the ironclad condition…"—*Down East, The Magazine of Maine*

J

jetsam: *cargo or equipment tossed overboard.* Often seen in the phrase, "flotsam and jetsam." "The port-labourers were of many nationalities and races…the flotsam and jetsam of the centuries of trade, piracy, wars and revolutions comprising the history of this keypoint on the Spanish Main…"—William H.S. Jones, *The Cape Horn Breed*

Jolly Roger: *the flag of a pirate ship, consisting of a white death's head (human skull) and crossbones with a black background.* Besides its present meaning of jovial or merry, "jolly" in the past had several slang meanings, among them "a royal marine" and "slightly drunk." "Roger," a man's name, has a vulgar meaning in Britain: to have sexual intercourse with a woman. "They could have fitted perfectly into a picture of buccaneers of the Spanish Main if they had only had red sashes about their waists, cutlasses in their belts, braces of pistols in their hands, and above them the Jolly Roger."—John Cameron, *John Cameron's Odyssey*

Judas lanterns: *false lights made to appear like the lights of a ship, to deceive sailors and lure ships to their destruction so that their cargo might be plundered.* Judas was the apostle who betrayed Jesus.

junk: *worthless scraps of glass, metal, etc., to be discarded; anything of inferior quality.* The term is nautical in origin and originally applied only to bits and pieces of rope that would be saved and, when time allowed (as often happened on a long voyage), spun into rope-yarn. "The owners of a vessel buy up incredible quantities of 'old junk,' which the sailors unlay, after drawing out the yarns, knot them together, and roll them up in balls. These 'rope yarns' are constantly used for various purposes, but the greater part is manufactured into spun yarn."—Richard Henry Dana, Jr., *Two Years Before the Mast*

jury-rigged: *constructed for temporary use, as in an emergency.* The adjective "jury" has the nautical meaning of "temporary." "Her masts, of course, would have gone overboard; but once the storm relaxed, it would have needed mere carpentry to step spars against their stumps, rig jury-sails, repair the rudder, and so limp home."— Richard Hughes, *In Hazard*

keel over: *to fall or faint from fatigue, shock, or overindulgence of alcohol*. A ship that has keeled over is one that has capsized. "The atmosphere chilled, a million hissing, shrieking demons seemed tearing through the rigging, the vessel keeled over until her lee bulwarks were buried in a green and white sea that poured in on deck."—Albert Sonnichsen, *Deep Sea Vagabonds*; "Our progress, unhappily, became slower and slower as one man after another keeled over and settled to the bottom of the boat, where he wallowed in sweet dreams and bilge water, till all were helpless. There was I with a drunken crew…"—John Cameron, *John Cameron's Odyssey*; "On hearing this I became faint and had to support myself to avoid keeling over. All about the foot of the mast blood was spattered from Jones' head; his skull had been smashed to a pulp."—ibid.

keelhaul: *to punish or castigate severely*. Keelhauling was a cruel and often fatal form of punishment, whereby the person was stripped, bound, slung at one end of the main-yard and dragged under the keel of the ship from one side to the other. If he didn't drown he might die or remain disfigured and crippled from the severe lacerations caused by the sharp barnacles attached to the hull. "…keel-hauling…consists of attaching tackles to the two extremities of the main-yard, and passing the rope under the ship's bottom. To one end of this rope the culprit is secured; his own shipmates are then made to run him up and down, first on this side, then on that—now scraping the ship's hull under water—anon, hoisted, stunned and breathless, into the air."—Herman Melville, *White-Jacket*; "Well I got a regular keelhauling for my pains, for the ship was lifting and pitching, so that before I could get fixed for a swim I was plunged under and jerked out of the water several times, that I was glad to cry quits and come on board again."—Edward Ely, *The Wanderings of Edward Ely*

keep company: *to court; woo.* Ships in a squadron "keep company" with one another. "On the eighth of October, a full day before the wind slackened, they sighted the whaleship *Massachusetts*...and made signals for her to keep company with them..."—Everett S. Allen, *Children of the Light*; "The two captains signaled to each other for more than an hour, and arranged to keep company during the night and burn blue lights occasionally as we were close on the South American coast off St. Salvador." —Edward Lacey, quoted in *Diaries from the Days of Sail*

Keep your weather eye open: *Be alert or on the lookout for trouble.* A "weather eye" is skilled at observing signs that the weather is changing. It is actually the eye exposed to bad weather (the direction from which the storm is driving rain, sleet, or whatever). The natural tendency is to close that eye—but that is the eye which should be kept open because it is facing the direction from which hazards—objects blown by the wind or borne by the current, etc.—are likely to come. "The water that blew in our eyes came with such force that it made them bloodshoten."—Charles Pierce, quoted in *Whaling Letters*; "During my next watch I was careful to keep my weather eye on the after companion-way door, and the slightest noise from the direction of his room caused me to beat a hasty retreat to the main deck."—Frederick Perry, *Fair Winds & Foul*; "I kept my weather eye open for a ship bound for deep water."—John Kenlon, *Fourteen Years A Sailor*; "The captain showed me the grave; I dug up the body, keeping a weather eye on Jacobson as I did so..."—John Cameron, *John Cameron's Odyssey*; "...how could I but lightly hold my obligations to observe all whale-ships' standing orders, 'Keep your weather eye open, and sing out every time.'"—Herman Melville, *Moby Dick*; "Old Jock, for once at any rate, had had his weather eye bedimmed."—David W. Bone, *The Brassbounder*

kiss (or **hug** or **marry**) **the gunner's daughter**: *to be flogged.* Men were often lashed to guns (cannons) when flogged. "I don't know what officers are made of now-a-days. I'll marry some of you young gentlemen to the gunner's daughter before long."—Frederick Marryat, *Peter Simple*

know the ropes: *to understand or have experience with the details of a procedure.* Rigging, attached to rows of belaying-pins, occupied the same relative position on all ships of a type, so that an experienced sailor, having memorized the order of the ropes, would know exactly which ones to seize hold of for a particular task. "The captain, who had been on the coast before, and knew the ropes, took the steering oar."—Richard Henry Dana, Jr., *Two Years Before the Mast*; "...there is such an infinite number of totally new names of new things to learn, that at first it seemed impossible for me to master them all. If you have ever seen a ship, you must have remarked what a thicket of ropes there are; and how they all seemed mixed and entangled together like a great skein of yarn."—Herman Melville, *Redburn*; "On shipboard the exact position of every rope had to be known so that a man could put his hand upon it as quickly in the darkness as in the daylight, and woe betide the poor sailor who was unfortunate enough to let go the wrong rope when obeying an order."—Frederick Perry, *Fair Winds & Foul*

L

laid up: *confined as an invalid.* From "laid up in ordinary," a term applied to a disused frigate. "Besides being over twenty years old she had been laid up on a mud-flat the last three years." —Albert Sonnichsen, *Deep Sea Vagabonds*; "We passed under the guns of rocky Alcatraz, and stood over to the wooded slopes and vineyards of Saucilito, where many 'laid-up' ships were lying at the buoys, with upper yards down and huge ballast booms lashed alongside."--David W. Bone, *The Brassbounder*

landmark: *an event that is a turning point in history.* Ships depended on prominent objects on shore (landmarks) for coastwise navigation. Sighting a familiar one was often the occasion for altering course. "North of us heavy masses of vapor, banked by the breeze, showed where the land lay, but no landmark, no feature of coast or headland, stood clear of the mist to guide us.—David W. Bone, *The Brassbounder*

lay of the land: *situation or arrangement.* A mariner approaching an unfamiliar coast would want to "see how the land lies," that is, determine its nature. "'It would have been a waste of time to hunt 'em; unpleasant as well, for we knew nothing of the lay of the land.'"—John Cameron, *John Cameron's Odyssey*

lazaret: *a ship's storeroom; a hospital treating contagious diseases;*

a hospital ship. Lazarus is the name of a diseased beggar in the sixteenth chapter of St. Luke. *Lazaret* entered English from the Italian *lazaretto*, meaning leper or beggar. "Supplies were commonly kept in the 'lazarette,' a belowdeck storage space right aft."—Julianna FreeHand, *A Seafaring Legacy*; "Joe was taken to the lazaret where he was kept until the captain came off and it was decided to send him ashore..."—Frederick Pease Harlow, *The Making of a Sailor*

limey (also **limejuicer**): *Englishman.* A slang term derived from the practice of issuing limes or lime juice to British sailors to prevent scurvy. "British ships are known the world over as Limejuicers, and this name is even applied to British seamen by Americans when speaking of them with contempt..."—Albert Sonnichsen, *Deep Sea Vagabonds;* "Thrown on his own resources and half starved, he managed to get enough work to live on the island for nearly three months and finally got away by shipping aboard the bark *Elora*, a lime-juicer, of Liverpool, England..."—Frederick Pease Harlow, *The Making of a Sailor*; "We had also an ample supply of West Indian limejuice, the compulsory ration on British ships, as a preventative of scurvy on long voyages...Because of this rule...the Americans called us 'limejuicers,' or 'limeys' for short."—William H.S. Jones, *The Cape Horn Breed*

lobster (or **lobster-back**): *a soldier or marine.* From the red uniform, similar in color to a boiled crustacean. "Paddy was as good as his word, for he took the rust off the marine so well he was forced to give in, and we were all happy to see the lobster-back's pride taken out of him."—John Nicol, *The Life and Adventures of John Nicol, Mariner*

long pig: *human flesh eaten by cannibals.* The term originated in the Fiji islands and was translated from the native language by British and American sailors. "The expression 'long pig' is not a joke, nor a phrase invented by the Europeans, but one frequently used by the Fijians, who looked upon a corpse as ordinary butcher meat, and called a human body *puaka balava*, long pig, in contradistinction to *puaka dina*, or real pig."—St. Johnston, *Camping Amongst Cannibals*; "If the blacks are hostile, they can easily ambush us and have a big feast of *long pig*—so human flesh was known to traders and blackbirders and perhaps to cannibals as well." —John Cameron, *John Cameron's Odyssey*; "Once in the hands of his fellow devils, he would have been put to excruciating torture; in the end roasted for breaking the chief's tabu. How the flesh of 'long pig' could be wholesome when the animal had undergone agony before being slaughtered perplexes me."—ibid.

long (or **shore**) **togs**: *a landman's clothes; clothes worn ashore, especially full dress clothes.* The word "tog," meaning coat or cloak, and by extension, clothing in general, derives from the Latin *toga*. "But I was not many days at sea, when I found that my shore clothing, or 'long togs,' as the sailors call them, were but ill adapted to the life I now led."—Herman Melville, *Redburn*; "It would be suggested that perhaps Jack would like to have a nice new suit of shore togs; and the new-found friend would immediately steer his sailor companion to some clothing shop, where they would proceed to fit Jack out 'from truck to keelson'..."—John Kenlon, *Fourteen Years A Sailor*; "The Dagos, after the manner of their kind, were polishing up their knives, and the 'white men' were brushing and airing their 'longshore togs' in readiness for a day that the gallant breeze was bringing nearer."—David W. Bone, *The Brassbounder*

loose cannon: *an unreliable person who, being privy to certain information, could, by revealing that information, cause damage to a cause or an organization; something dangerously out of control.* A loose cannon rolling about on a ship at sea, particularly during a naval battle, is a dangerous object indeed. "One of our guns was overcharged and jumped across the deck..."—Thomas Garry Fraser, *Captain Fraser's Voyages*

lose one's bearings: *to become lost or confused—often used metaphorically. (To get one's bearings would be to discover the* *right course of action.)* A bearing is an angular direction measured from one position to another. Ships would often use landmarks to obtain their bearings. "Not that I was weak or gallied, but I just felt like keeping still for a while so as to sort of get my bearings, so I went home to the Vineyard and I spent the winter there."—George Fred Tilton, *"Cap'n George Fred" Himself*

lose the number of one's mess: *(naval slang for) to be killed.* "'I'm afeard, doctor, I'll soon be losing the number of my mess!' (a sea phrase, for departing this life) and he closed his eyes, and moaned."—Herman Melville, *Omoo*; "White-Jacket, for one, was a long time rapt in calculations, concerning the various 'numbers' allotted him by the...First Lieutenant. In the first place, White-Jacket was given the *number of his mess*; then his *ship's number*, or the number to which he must answer when the watch-roll is called; then the number of his hammock; then, the number of the gun to which he was assigned; besides a variety of other numbers..."—Herman Melville, *White-Jacket*; "The common seamen in a large frigate are divided into some thirty or forty messes, put down on the purser's books as Mess No. 1, Mess No. 2, Mess No. 3, &c. The members of each mess club their rations of provisions, and breakfast, dine, and sup together..."—Herman Melville, *White-Jacket*

mainstay: *that which can be chiefly relied upon; principal support.* From the name for the strong rope that stays, or supports, the mainmast. "With the help of the buntlines, leech-lines and spilling-lines, some of the wind was smothered from the sail but there was a flapping of canvas about the mainstay that shook the whole ship in a tremor."—Frederick Pease Harlow, *The Making of a Sailor*

make both ends meet: *to get by (in the economic sense); to manage to live within one's means.* On long voyages ropes, upon which so much depended, often became scarce: damaged or lost in foul weather. The torn ends of broken ropes would be pulled together and spliced.

make headway: *to move forward; make progress.* From the head (forepart) of a ship. "We were making good headway to the westward, tacking only about every twelve hours, and were heading inshore to pick up, if possible, the snow- and ice-clad peak of the Cape to verify our reckoning."—Frederick Perry, *Fair Winds & Foul*; "Having lost our headway, we now fell off into the trough of the sea and swiftly and surely began to drift straight back toward those dangerous cliffs that we were trying so hard to avoid."—ibid.; "There was no jib or any kind of a head sail and I doubt that she could make any headway with the wind forward of the beam, therefore, she could not beat to windward."—William Fish

Williams, quoted in *One Whaling Family*; "Although awkward with the bucket and swab, yet I made pretty good headway towards the last and when four bells struck I had only one side of the cabin to do."—Frederick Pease Harlow, *The Making of a Sailor*

make heavy weather of: *to exaggerate the difficulty of a task to be completed.* A ship experiencing heavy (severe) weather would have to struggle to make headway, or even to stay afloat.

make sternway: *to go backwards.* From the stern, or rear part, of a ship.

Man overboard!: *Someone has fallen from the ship into the sea.* The conciseness of the expression says it all. "'Man overboard!' There is something in that cry that penetrates through a ship in the hardest roaring of a gale."—Thomas Garry Fraser, *Captain Fraser's Voyages*; "Instantly the much dreaded cry 'man overboard' was raised."—Jon Kenlon, *Fourteen Years A Sailor*; "Instantly, there was the cry of 'Man overboard'; the Old Man ordered the helm down, and, springing to the rack, threw a lifebuoy from the starboard quarter; the Second Mate, not seeing him throw it, threw another from the port."—David W. Bone, *The Brassbounder*; "'Man overboard!' It was the inevitable cry, but of no avail whatsoever, and every man knew it. If Henderson had not been instantly killed when he struck the water, he was in any case lost and gone forever."—William H.S. Jones, *The Cape Horn Breed*

manhandle: *to treat roughly; physically abuse.* Originally, the term meant to move heavy cargo by hand, when mechanical means were lacking. "Changing the complete suit of sails requires the manhandling of every stitch of canvas, and every rope, wire or tackle with which they are set."—William H. S. Jones, *The Cape Horn Breed*; "…while standing out of harm's way, the valiant captain danced up and down with a whale-pike, calling upon his officers to manhandle that atrocious scoundrel, and smoke him along to the quarter deck."—Herman Melville, *Moby Dick*; "This often proved a successful bait and secured Captain Carney a crew when all other efforts failed owing to his evil reputation as a man-handler."—Henry H. Bootes, *Deep-Sea Bubbles*

maroon: *to abandon or forsake someone utterly.* Pirates or others who set a person ashore on a deserted island were said to "maroon" him. The term comes, through French, from the Spanish for fugitive slave.

midshipman's nuts: *pieces of broken biscuit.* Such pieces would be hard, like nuts. "The American sailors mess on the deck, and peck up their broken biscuit, or *midshipmen's nuts*, like fowls in a barnyard."—Herman Melville, *White-Jacket*; "Accordingly I took a double handful of those small, broken, flinty bits of biscuit which generally go by the name of 'midshipmen's nuts' and thrust them into the bosom of my frock..."—Herman Melville, *Typee*

mooncusser (also **mooncurser**): *wrecker; plunderer; someone who lures vessels to destruction in order to loot them.* The term also is sometimes applied to those who merely take advantage of a wreck by salvaging whatever washes up on shore. "Wild stories used to be told of the wreckers of the Cape, who decoyed ships ashore by the use of false lights. Mooncussers they were called, because the moon interfered with their business, and they cursed it."—Edwin Valentine Mitchell, *It's an Old Cape Cod Custom*; "Meanwhile the thirsty inhabitants of Provincetown had already got wind of the disaster, and even then were raiding the *Spindler*. This enraged the captain, who rushed out of the Coast Guard quarters and threw two of the 'mooncussers' off the vessel and down on the sand."—Edward Rowe Snow, *A Pilgrim Returns to Cape Cod*

Mother Carey's chickens: *storm petrels.* Why these birds of the sea are so named is not known; it may be from the Latin *Mater Cara*, "Dear Mother," for the Virgin Mary, who is the patron saint of sailors. As with the albatross, killing one of Mother Carey's chickens results in extremely bad luck, including the likelihood of drowning.

"The last one that we caught the artist took into the cabin to make a drawing of it. It was very tame, and remained for a quarter of an hour without struggling, loosely held in the hand until its portrait was secured, when it was permitted to rejoin its companions. Like all those we captured, it had a singularly gentle and innocuous expression, and its resemblance in this respect to a young chicken was so great that we were satisfied of the appropriateness of the term chicken commonly applied to the bird by sailors—though why it should be called Mother Carey's is an unsolved mystery."—Robert Carter, *A Summer Cruise on the Coast of New England*

mug up: *to drink coffee together.* Originally, the term was more general, meaning "to eat," and apparently originated with the Grand Banks schooners.

Nantucket sleigh-ride: *the dragging of a boat by a harpooned whale.* Under such circumstances a boat might reach a speed of thirty knots or more; the ride could end in death or severe injury to the crew (not to mention the whale). Nantucket was noted for its whaling. "When a whale tried to run away from the pain by sounding and then making off, it dragged the boat along in what was romantically called a 'Nantucket sleigh ride.'"—Joan Druett, *"She Was a Sister Sailor"*; "This kind of sleigh-ride was often at railroad speed and was perhaps one of the most exhilarating and exciting experiences in the line of sport. An empty boat would certainly capsize, but a whaleboat had six trained, strong, athletic men sitting on her thwarts, whose skill enabled them to sway their bodies to the motion of the boat so that she would keep an even keel, even though her speed might plough small valleys over the huge swells and across the broad troughs of an angry ocean, and great billows of foam piled up at her bow while the water rushed past the stern like a mad whirlpool."—*Whale Fishery of New England*; "Before we could get into action, the whale started to run and we were off on a 'Nantucket sleigh ride,' but it was not very fast."—William Fish Williams, quoted in *One Whaling Family*; "Presently, a dark object swam out; the line began to straighten; then smoked round the loggerhead, and, quick as thought, the boat sped like an arrow through the water. They were 'fast,' and the whale was running."— Herman Melville, *Omoo*; "If the whale runs the line will be held by a turn around the loggerhead so that the boat will have to be towed along behind him. This is what they call a 'Nantucket sleigh ride,' although the Lord only knows what Nantucket has to do with it any more than any other place."—George Fred Tilton, *"Cap'n George Fred" Himself*

night hawk: *a long black pennant which, when hoisted, signaled to passing ships that the ship flying it was homeward bound and willing to take mail or messages.* From its resemblance to the bird.

nor'easter: *a violent storm that blows from the northeast.* Those of us who live in New England, especially on Cape Cod, have experienced quite a few.

no room to swing a cat: *(a description of a place with) insufficient space.* The cat referred to is the infamous cat-o'-nine-tails, the whip used aboard ships for flogging sailors. It had nine "tails"—knotted cords that left marks on human flesh like the deep scratches inflicted by a cat. The areas below deck were confined, so floggings took place on deck, where there was sufficient room to swing a cat-o'-nine-tails.

O

Old Hallett!: *(whalemen's cry signifying and celebrating the completion of the cutting up of a whale for processing).* (origin unknown). "When the last piece of blubber comes on deck, it is customary for all hands to yell, 'Hurray for five and forty more!' or 'Old Hallett!' Captain George Fred Tilton, who said he had hollered 'Old Hallett!' more times for more years than he could remember, confessed that he had not the faintest notion who Hallett was or why the whalemen yelled it."—Everett S. Allen, *Children of the Light*

old salt: *an experienced sailor.* "Salt," by association with salt water, is a jocular term for sailor. "The captain…was a typical old salt, having spent forty-five years of his life in sail, during thirty-five of which he was the master."—Frederick Perry, *Fair Winds & Foul*; "The old salts now began to tell us younger men stories of running the terrible Easting down, all in a highly tragic vein."—Albert Sonnichsen, *Deep Sea Vagabonds*; "He has donned the familiar old red flannel shirt that he stands his wheel in, and bareheaded as he always is at sea, he looks a typical old salt…"—David W. Bone, *The Brassbounder*

on an even keel: *balanced; steady on one's feet.* A steady ship is on an even keel. "Working rapidly, the crew members cut away the masts and debris, and were thankful to find that the *Essex* was able to come back to an even keel, although she was waterlogged and actually a floating hulk."—Edward Rowe Snow, *A Pilgrim Returns to Cape Cod*; "The whole cargo had to be stored and blocked off so that it could not shift, no matter how heavily the ship might roll or pitch during the voyage, and at the same time it had to keep her on an even keel and properly trimmed."—Frederick Perry, *Fair Winds & Foul*

on deck: *present; waiting to take one's turn (for example, a batter in the game of baseball).* From the days of sailing ships, when seamen would be called to the deck for action (work or warfare). "In watch below we were assured of our rest, and even when 'on deck'…were at liberty to seek out a soft plank and lie back, gazing up at the gently swaying mastheads till sleep came again."—David W. Bone, *The Brassbounder*

on (one's) beam ends: *in a hazardous situation; in the last extremity of desperation.* A ship listing so far that her beams (horizontal timbers that run at right angles to the keel) are vertical with the water (and the ship is in danger of capsizing) is "on her beam ends." "The little brig was close-hauled upon the wind, and lying over, as it then seemed to me, nearly upon her beam ends." —Richard Henry Dana, Jr., *Two Years Before the Mast*; "In the next instant, a wilderness of foam hurled us upon our beam-ends, and, rushing over us fore and aft, swept the entire decks from stem to stern."— Edgar Allan Poe, "MS. Found in a Bottle"; "…the squall…was upon us. It struck us on our starboard side and the ship was on her beam ends in a moment."—Edward Ely, *The Wanderings of Edward Ely*; "The barque was on her beam ends, rolling about in a long northerly swell, and the lower yards were almost dipping into the water on the low side as she rolled."—Sir James Bisset, *Sail Ho!*

on the rocks: *in a state of ruin.* Many a ship has struck rocks and as a consequence been broken up and sunk. "My cot was swung immediately on my arrival, but we lay three days longer than was expected in the harbor, riding out a gale of wind, which broke the chain cables of both ships, and drove several merchant vessels on the rocks."—Nathaniel Parker Willis, *A Summer Cruise in the Mediterranean*; "We were going on the rocks less than ten hours after leaving Liverpool."—John Kenlon, *Fourteen Years A Sailor*

on the wrong tack: *following a wrong course of action.* "Tack" in this instance refers to the position of a ship relative to the trim of its sails. "We are still on the wrong tack. Yesterday we were WSW and only gained 10 miles on the right course; today we are running ESE and have not gained a mile in the right direction."—Edward Lacey, quoted in *Diaries from the Days of Sail*

out of commission: *not in working condition.* The term was originally applied only to an inactive man-of-war.

out of one's depth: *beyond one's expertise or capacity to understand.* Here, the metaphorical meaning of "depth"—understanding—has superseded the literal (physical) meaning.

overhaul: *to go over thoroughly for needed repairs; to take apart in order to make repairs.* To be worked upon, a ship's rigging first had to be hauled over (overhauled) into position. During this process the rigging would be examined and, if necessary, repaired.

P

Paddy's hurricane: *a dead calm.* Paddy is the nickname for an Irishman. "A dead calm was known as 'Paddy's hurricane.'"—Sir James Bisset, *Sail Ho!*; "This is essentially one of Paddy's Hurricanes. There is no wind, yet it is not exactly calm, it neither blows from one point of the compass yet neither three or four but we have an occasional puff from all points."—Edward Ely, *The Wanderings of Edward Ely*; "At times wind-jammers are favored by what sailors term 'Paddy's Hurricane,' that is, the wind blows up and down the mast."—John Kenlon, *Fourteen Years A Sailor*; "…but by actual observation it struck us that the winds here never blew at all, or, after the manner of Paddy's hurricane, up and down."—Albert Sonnichsen, *Deep Sea Vagabonds*

paying homage to Neptune: *vomiting while seasick.* In Roman mythology, Neptune was the god of the sea. In poetic usage, Neptune has come to represent the ocean. This humorous reference to vomiting was probably the creation of classically educated passengers or officers rather than of the common seamen.

pier-head jump: *someone who joins the crew of a ship at the very last moment, after it has set sail. Also, the act of so joining (or deserting) a ship.* The expression derives from the fact that the person (often someone desperate to escape the law or other pursuers) would literally jump from the head of the pier onto the ship as it sailed by. "Sheering cautiously out of the fairway, we come to anchor at Tail of the Bank to wait for our 'pier-head jumps.'"—David W. Bone, *The Brassbounder*; "He—of us all—had come to sea 'same as he was goin' to church!' A pier-head jump!"—ibid.; "He had come on board at Greenock—a pier-head jump, with his wardrobe on his back and a 'hauf-mutchkin' of very inferior whisky in his pocket."—ibid.; "With the call of the watch, the mate could only round up Hans, Andy and Jim Dunn. All the other members of the crew had made a pier-head jump during the night."—Frederick Pease Harlow, *The Making of a Sailor*; "Some in desperation would make a 'pierhead jump,' that is, they would wait at the end of the pier to jump on board if the Mate beckoned to them if he needed another man or two."—Sir James Bisset, *Sail Ho!*

pilot: *someone who flies an airplane*. A pilot is the person who guides a ship into port (often a local person familiar with the waters, and not a member of the ship's company). The term derives from *peil-loth*, a word for "lead line" (sounding line). *Peil-loth* ultimately derives from the ancient Greek for rudder or steering oar. "It was the famous pilot, Juan Fernandes, immortalized by the island named after him, who put an end to these coasting tribulations, by boldly venturing the experiment—as De Gama did before him with respect to Europe—of standing broad out from land."—Herman Melville, *The Encantadas*; "The American consul, in a smart boat, came alongside before the *Spray* reached the breakwater, and a young naval officer, who feared for the safety of my vessel, boarded, and offered his services as pilot."—Joshua Slocum, *Sailing Alone Around the World*

pipe one's eyes: *to weep*. The origin of this expression is "to pipe away," an allusion to the boatswain's whistle. "'But I say, Jonathan, my lad, don't pipe your eye now about the loss of your crown…'"—Herman Melville, *White-Jacket*

plane sailing: *easy and uncomplicated (after a strenuous course)*. When setting a course on the open seas, navigators had to take into account the earth's curvature. If they failed to do so they risked ending up off course, perhaps a continent or two away from their intended destination. But when after days, months, or even years of traversing the ocean they finally neared their goal they could ignore the world's rotundity. Charts used for sailing along coasts, since they represented only a tiny portion of the earth's surface, could project a course on a geometric plane. Hence the expression, "It's all plane sailing now." (The phrase is often inaccurately written as "plain" sailing.) "The *Spray* had now passed nearly all the dangers of the Coral Sea and Torres Strait, which, indeed, were not a few; and all ahead from this point was plain sailing and a straight course."—Joshua Slocum, *Sailing Alone Around the World*

plum-puddinger: *a small whaler making short voyages.* On such a voyage, the crew would be fed on fresh provisions, including an abundance of plum pudding. "A plum-pudding voyage was confined to Atlantic waters, and plum-puddingers never knew sultry seas and barbarous coasts…"—Eleanor Early, *An Island Patchwork*; "After sitting a long time listening to the long stories of some sailors who had just come from a plum-pudding voyage, as they called it (that is, a short whaling-voyage in a schooner or brig, confined to the north of the line, in the Atlantic Ocean only); after listening to these plum-puddingers till nearly eleven o'clock, I went upstairs to bed…"—Herman Melville, *Moby Dick*

pull the dead horse: *to work for wages already paid.* "Seamen, on signing articles, sometimes get pay in advance, and they celebrate the term of the period thus paid for by dragging a canvas horse, stuffed with straw, round the deck and dropping him into the sea amidst cheers."—J.S. Farmer and W.E. Henley, *Slang and Its Analogues*; "'Why, dead 'orse is the first month out when you're working to pay off yer debt with yer boarding-house master—the crimps… 'E draws yew first month's wages from the shippin' agents the very day your ship sails with yew on board.'"—Hiram P. Bailey, *Shanghaied out of 'Frisco in the 'Nineties*; "But I can give you no money! Cotton to that! Yer know you hev not worked off all yer dead horse yet."—ibid.; "The Dead Horse Funeral solemnized the end of the month, of that first long month the wages of which had been squandered before the *Ida* left her wharf in Glasgow."—John Cameron, *John Cameron's Odyssey*; "'Dead 'oss is the fust month out, w'en ye're workin' for ye'r boardin'-mawster. 'E gets yer month's advawnce we'n ye sails, an' ye've got to work that hoff afore ye earns any pay!'"—David W. Bone, *The Brassbounder*; "The meaning of the present ceremony is, when the crew join on, they are given a month's advance of their wages, which they have to work out; this the sailors dub their 'dead horse.' The month being now up, hence the ceremony and celebration. At the end the old horse is thrown overboard, and round upon round of cheers are given—*which of course earns a tot of rum*."—W.H. Angel, *The Clipper Ship "Sheila"*

pump ship: *to make water (urinate); vomit.* The analogy of emptying the bladder to pumping water from ships (which often leaked badly) is obvious. "I went forr'd to pump ship when they were clearing the cables, and the master's sampan was below. The coolie had a pan of rice for his breakfast: there floated a great dollop out of the hole and it went into the rice. All the hands laughed but it made him swear!"—from the diary of Alexander Whitehead, quoted in *Diaries from the Days of Sail*

put in for: *to apply for; make a bid for.* A ship "puts in for" a harbor or port when entering it. "If further cause were needed to justify the serious course of 'putting in,' they had it when the carpenter reported water in the forepeak; and it was discovered that the broken jibboom had not hammered at the bows for nothing."—David W. Bone, *The Brassbounder*

put (or **shove**) **one's oar in**: *to meddle; interfere.* One can only imagine the nautical entanglements that led to this expression. "Now, needless to say, I intended such a casual personal remark for the ear of Ben alone; but somehow the negro cook caught it. What

possessed him to 'put in his oar' I do not know; but he did."—
Hiram P. Bailey, *Shanghaied out of 'Frisco in the 'Nineties*

raise the wind: *to borrow (or procure) money.* Although the wind in this phrase probably refers to wind in the sails of a ship, it may also refer to wind needed to set the grindstone of a mill in motion. "If his terms were hard, his money was good, and, excepting for the Old Man's grudging advances, we had no other way of 'raising the wind.'"—David W. Bone, *The Brassbounder*

rakish: *dashing; jaunty; debonair.* The term was originally applied to ships (especially pirate ships) that had a streamlined appearance because their masts were "raked" (slanted, inclined at an angle). "A brig! The very word summoned up the idea of a black, sea-worn craft, with high, cozy bulwarks, and rakish masts and yards."—Herman Melville, *Redburn*; "The officers said she was either a pirate or a slaver. Her hull was long low & black & her masts much raking."—John T. Perkins, quoted in *"She Was a Sister Sailor"* by Joan Druett; "However, I went and bought a peaked badge cap, of rakish design…and wore it well on the side of my head, in the approved fashion of smart young second mates of that period."—Sir James Bisset, *Sail Ho!*

reefer: *a marijuana cigarette.* To reef is to shorten a sail by tucking in a portion and rolling it around a yard (spar). (The double-breasted jacket known as a reefer gets its name from the midshipmen who customarily wore it. They were called reefers because one of their duties was reefing—rolling up a portion of sail and tying it down.)

rest on one's oars: *to stop working; to desist from trying*. Rowing is hard work, and often requires will as well as effort.

roaring forties: *the degrees of latitude between 40 degrees and 50 degrees North—the most tempestuous part of the Atlantic*. (The term was also sometimes applied to the same zone in the South Atlantic.) This nautical expression may have suggested the epithet given to the decade in the twentieth century known as "the roaring twenties." "The SE trades would last until about 35 deg. S, the region of the 'roaring forties.'"—Sir James Bisset, *Sail Ho!*; "From Latitude 50 degrees South we made good progress to the northward through the Roaring Forties, which at this season are known as the 'Variables of Capricorn.'"—William H.S. Jones, *The Cape Horn Breed*

rock the boat: *to engage in reckless behavior likely to ruin an enterprise*. A boat is easily upset. Passengers and crew must remain as still as possible lest by their motion (rocking) they upset it.

rounding the Horn: *sailing around Cape Horn (a headland on an island of Tierra del Fuego, Chile, the southernmost point of South America)*. Before the Panama Canal was constructed, ships sailing from the east coast to the west coast of America, and the return, had to sail around Cape Horn. "The nautical term 'rounding the Horn' means passing from fifty degrees south in the Atlantic to fifty degrees in the Pacific."—Frederick Perry, *Fair Winds & Foul*; "The steward had it from the captain that we were rounding the Horn. My preconceived ideas of rounding the Horn were somewhat altered."—Albert Sonnichsen, *Deep Sea Vagabonds*; "In the middle of the yard Paddy set up a ram's horn, and about this the men were marched, a procedure that enabled Paddy truthfully to assure a captain that the 'seamen' had been around the Horn no end of times."—John Cameron, *John Cameron's Odyssey*; "Rounding Cape Horn from the eastward, setting to the teeth of the great west wind, to the shock and onset of towering seas; furious combination of the elements that sweep unchecked around the globe!"—David W. Bone, *The Brassbounder*

rummage: *to search thoroughly (sometimes frantically and clumsily) through a drawer, chest, cupboard, etc.* The term, which derives from Latin by way of Norman French, originally referred to the storage of cargo in a ship's hold.

run up the jib: *to cause to move or progress freely.* The jib boom is a spar that forms a continuation of the bowsprit.

S

sail close to the wind: *to live dangerously (or frugally); to pursue a doubtful course of action*. "Close to" in this expression means "against." Sailing against the wind, of course, is difficult, and can be dangerous, requiring a series of zigzags or tacks.

sail under false colors: *to pretend to be what one is not*. Pirate ships would often fly a false flag in order to deceive potential prey.

salt horse: *salted beef*. The salted beef served to sailors was not of the best quality and may have seemed like the meat of an old horse. However, the term originates from the fact that salt beef was periodically removed from storage and dumped into a cask for use by the cook. The cask was secured to the deck by means of four horseshoes attached to its sides. "By boiling them all day, and then working them over in a stew with gravy, rice pepper and other condiments, they are made tolerably palatable and are an improvement on Salt Horse."—George Henry Preble, *The Opening of Japan*; "'Old Horse' & 'Hard-bread' is the standing bill of fare!"—Enoch Carter Cloud, *Enoch's Voyage: Life on a Whale Ship*; "We had salt horse dough and yams for our dinner, but the latter were all bad."—from the diary of Alexander Whitehead, quoted in *Diaries from the Days of Sail*; "Our dinner consisted of a slab of salt beef, familiarly called 'salt horse,' some broken hardtack soaked in boiling water, a slab of bread and cup of coffee."—Walter

Hammond, *Mutiny on the* Pedro Varela; "Betwixt the mainmast and the pumps, / My body lies cut up in salt junks; / If you don't believe my story to be true, / Just go to the harness cask and you'll find my shoe."—W.H. Angel, *The Clipper Ship "Sheila"*

schooner: *a large beer glass.* The schooner is a small sea-going fore-and-aft rigged vessel once popular in America, especially in New England. The first schooner was launched in Gloucester, Massachusetts, in 1713 by Captain Andrew Robinson. The word is believed to derive from the Scots *scoon* (to glide or skim over water). "Schooner" in reference to a beer glass was originally "a three-masted schooner," i.e., larger than the average two-masted schooner. "She was schooner-rigged—that is, had two masts, and fore and aft sails."—Charles Nordhoff, *Whaling and Fishing*; "As the bos'un observed in the open sun on the fo'c'sle head: 'Not enough wind to blow the froth off a schooner of ale!'"—Hiram P. Bailey, *Shanghaied out of 'Frisco in the 'Nineties*; "No money—not even the price of a 'schooner!' And the ghost of nigh six months' salt beef, waiting to be 'laid!'"—David W. Bone, *The Brassbounder*

scouse: *lobscouse, a type of stew.* "The cook had just made for us a mess of hot 'scouse'—that is, biscuit pounded fine, salt beef cut into small pieces, and a few potatoes boiled up together and seasoned with pepper. This was a rare treat…"—Richard Henry Dana, Jr., *Two Years Before the Mast*; "The scouse is a curious mixture, onions, pepper, potatoes, several kinds of meat & everything eatable on the ship."—John T. Perkins, quoted in *"She Was a Sister Sailor"* by Joan Druett; "Supper consisted of a cup of tea, which had to be drunk quickly to prevent its eating a hole through the cup, the usual slab of bread and 'baked scouse.' This latter dish was nothing more than our noon meal, salt horse, and soaked hardtack, but this time the two ingredients were mixed together and the water evaporated off by baking."—Walter Hammond, *Mutiny on the* Pedro Varela

scuttlebutt: *gossip; inside information.* The cask on a ship in which the day's supply of drinking water was kept was known as the scuttlebutt ("scuttle" meaning a small hatch, and "butt" meaning cask). Just as workers in an office today tend to gather around the water bubbler to chat and exchange gossip, so did sailors around the scuttlebutt. "There is no part of the frigate where you will see more goings and comings of strangers, and overhear more greetings and gossipings of acquaintances, than in the immediate vicinity of the scuttle-butt, just forward of the main-hatchway, on the gundeck. The scuttle-butt is a goodly, round, painted cask, standing on end, and with its upper head removed, showing a narrow, circular shelf within, where rest a number of tin cups for the accommodation of drinkers."—Herman Melville, *White-Jacket*; "In 'tween-decks' was a scuttlebutt, holding fifteen barrels, which held the water supply used by the crew." —George Fred Tilton, *"Cap'n George Fred" Himself*

sea language: *swearing; profanity.* Sailors have a reputation for using strong language. "This proposition staggered me, and I am afraid that I expressed in violent sea language my opinion of his religion."—Thomas Garry Fraser, *Captain Fraser's Voyages*

sea-lawyer: *a shark.* (This opprobrious epithet dates back to at least 1810.) Also, *a captious or argumentative sailor.* "Whenever I found I had a sea-lawyer among them, I got rid of him as soon as possible— giving him a chance to desert."—Raphael Semmes, *Memoirs of Service Afloat During the War Between the States*; "He could 'hand, reef and steer' and was somewhat of a sea lawyer in his ability to keep himself out of trouble while slyly encouraging others to assert their rights and thereby get into trouble."—William Fish Williams, quoted in *One Whaling Family*; "'Go to hell, ye blasted sea-lawyer, you can't scare us with no blooming law-books.'"—Albert Sonnichsen, *Deep Sea Vagabonds*

seaman's disgrace: *a foul anchor.* No seaman worth his salt would foul an anchor.

second-rate: *not of the best quality.* From the classification of the five sizes, or rates, of British ships of war.

see the point: *to understand (the essential matter or purpose of a story or argument).* The mariner's compass card is divided into thirty-two equal divisions or points. A novice lacking nautical skills might, while at the helm (especially in foul weather), fail to see the point.

shanghai: *to forcibly recruit (i.e., kidnap) a sailor from port for service aboard a ship (often by the use of alcohol or drugs).* Shanghai in China was an unpopular destination with sailors; they had to be abducted in order to serve on a ship bound for that port. "Shanghai," though, is probably used for the China trade in general. The term originated on San Francisco's Barbary Coast. "'Now I didn't want to see nice fellows like you in the hands of fellows who would shanghai you.'"—Thomas Garry Fraser, *Captain Fraser's Voyages*; "Every ship got a percentage of landsmen shanghaied on board, drugged and drunk."—ibid.; "SHANGHAIED—Taken to sea without consulting the person taken; usually accomplished by 'dopeing' (drugging) the victim."—Hiram P. Bailey, *Shanghaied out of 'Frisco in the 'Nineties*; "Here was a man who had been outrageously used. Drugged—robbed—'shanghaied!'"—David W. Bone, *The Brassbounder*

shellback: *an experienced or veteran sailor; a tough, knowledgeable old salt.* So called because he was hardened by experience, or perhaps because barnacles and other sea creatures had sufficient time to grow on his back. "I was surprised, for the five were all hard old shellbacks who were notorious stickers (i.e., indifferent sailors and workers, but who stuck to a good ship...)"—Thomas Garry Fraser, *Captain Fraser's Voyages*; "Yes, and there the old shellback stood, legs apart to the swing of the ship, his watery blue eyes in the sombre light of the forecastle twinkling and twinkling with deep merriment."—Hiram P. Bailey, *Shanghaied out of 'Frisco in the 'Nineties*; "Shore folks have the idea we're a lot of old water-logged, barnacle-covered shellbacks, always hitching our trousers and chewing plug tobacco."—Albert Sonnichsen, *Deep Sea Vagabonds*

shipshape: *neat; orderly; tidy.* A reference to the orderly rigging of old sailing ships. "We soon had her in shipshape again, with bad-weather sails bent, for we were now approaching the regions of the Great West Wind."—Albert Sonnichsen, *Deep Sea Vagabonds*

shipshape and Bristol fashion: *spick-and-span.* In the early days of sailing Bristol, England, was famed as a major port. "They said her decks were as white as snow—holystoned every morning, like a man-of-war's; everything on board 'shipshape and Bristol-fashion.'"—Richard Henry Dana, Jr., *Two Years Before the Mast*; "'A place for everything, an' everybody 'as 'is place, I says!... That's shipshape an' Bristol fashion, ain't it?'"—David W. Bone, *The Brassbounder*; "We were kept busy...polishing brass and woodwork; and doing anything else that the ingenuity of the Mates could find to keep the crew from idleness and to make the vessel shipshape and Bristol fashion..."—Sir James Bisset, *Sail Ho!*

shipshape and sailor fashion: *neat and orderly.* This variation on the above expression is a testament to the habitual cleanliness of most ships and their crews. "We left the bay of San Francisco...the 2nd of Aug, and the ship's company were all day engaged in cleaning the ship and putting things to right in ship shape and sailor fashion."—Edward Ely, *The Wanderings of Edward Ely*; "Some insolence from the bully soon gave Stewart his opportunity; he sailed in and dressed the man in shipshape fashion."—John Cameron, *John Cameron's Odyssey*; "A few pieces of old chain were put in to weight him down, all ship-shape and sailor fashion, and when it was done we laid him out on the main hatch with the Flag he had served cast over him."—David W. Bone, *The Brassbounder*

Shiver my timbers! *an exclamation denoting shock or surprise.* The timbers of a ship that violently strikes a rock or other object will surely shiver. This expression may be more the invention of literary authors than an actual utterance used by sailors. "Then we don't 'shiver our timbers' or shout 'ship ahoy!' when we see a friend coming down the street. Not on your life. We leave that to amateur yachtsmen."—Albert Sonnichsen, *Deep Sea Vagabonds;* "After Mick Mulligan had finished his yarn, our Finn seaman, Yonny Helsing, said, 'Shiver my timbers, Mick, dat vas a close shave.'"—Sir James Bisset, *Sail Ho!*

shove off: *(slang) to leave.* A boat is pushed away from (shoved off) a wharf, shore, or ship, by hand, oar, or other implement.

show your true colors: *to reveal your real nature.* It was customary, upon meeting another vessel or entering a harbor, for a ship to hoist its flag. Pirates or others wishing to deceive would hoist a false flag ("colors"), hoisting their true flag (in the case of pirates, the Jolly Roger) only at the last moment.

sister sailor: *a wife (usually of the captain) who accompanied her husband on a sea voyage.* This term was most customarily applied by the women themselves. "…the whaling wives had it much, much worse than their sister sailors on merchant ships, probably because of the eternal stench of rancid oil that oozed up from the bilges."—Joan Druett, *Hen Frigates*

skylark: *to frolic or engage in pranks.* From the behavior of sailors fooling around or "carrying on" in the rigging or tops of sails. "…by the term skylarking is meant wrestling, sparring, playing in the rigging, other athletic sports and boisterous pastimes by which sailors avoid boredom and release their energy."—Daniel Weston Hall, *Arctic Rovings*; "At length he told them if he saw any more such skylarking, that he would fetch them out of that, and they might have a trial of the forecastle for their fun."—Edward Ely, *The Wanderings of Edward Ely*; "Hickerty and Helman were skylarking at teatime and Hickerty's knife stuck in Helman's leg. Helman is laid up."—from the diary of Alexander Whitehead,

skyscraper: *a tall building.* From the sailor's name for a small triangular sail which, in very fair weather, was hoisted at the tip of the topmost mast. It was also referred to as a "moon-raker" or "star-chaser." "But I have heard that some ships carry still smaller sails, above the skysail, called moon-sails, and sky-scrapers, and cloud-rakers."—Herman Melville, *Redburn*; "We could have raised another sail over the skysail, a moon-raker, but take it for all in all, the extra help that it would have given was not worth the expenditure of rope for halyards, sheets, and clewlines, to reach so high as the skysail-mast for so short a run…"—W.H. Angel, *The Clipper Ship "Sheila"*

slip one's cable: *to die.* This is a variation of 'slip one's moorings.' "…though doubtless the original Samuel must long ago have slipped his cable for the great South Sea of the other world."—Herman Melville, *Moby Dick*

slip one's moorings: *to die.* Moorings are equipment such as anchors or chains that hold a ship fast. "A slight blow on the nose with a club was sufficient to 'slip their moorings' and in 30 minutes we had them on the ship's deck, skinned & ready for use!"—Enoch Carter Cloud, *Enoch's Voyage: Life on a Whale Ship*; "I would rather 'slip my moorings' tonight than be informed that the time will come when I will be dead to the holy influence of Dear Parents & Sisters at home!"—ibid.

slush fund: *money raised by a group for an undesignated purpose; a fund raised by a political group for illegal purposes, such as bribery.* Slush, the name for grease or fat collected from the pots on naval ships, belonged to the cook, and was usually sold to the purser to be made into candles. "'I'll sign all right at top wages with privileges of shakings and slush money as bonus…'"—Frederick Perry, *Fair Winds & Foul*; "Yet hunger drove the men to eat the lean portions; the fat—four fifths of the meat—went to the slush barrel, the contents of which, except for the oil used in our teapot lamps in the forecastle, were the cook's perquisite."—John Cameron, *John Cameron's Odyssey*

soft berth: *sinecure; cushy job.* A "berth" is a position of employment on a ship. "I figured that with my experience I might be able to hold some kind of a berth, but I had the idea that any man in the government service must be right up to scratch, and I didn't aim very high."—George Fred Tilton, *"Cap'n George Fred" Himself*

soldier: *to shirk one's duty.* "'Soger' (soldier) is the worst term of reproach that can be applied to a sailor. It signifies a *skulk*, a *shirk*— one who is always trying to get clear of work, and is out of the way, or hanging back, when duty is to be done…To make a sailor shoulder a handspike and walk fore and aft the deck like a sentry is the most ignominious punishment that could be put upon him. Such a punishment inflicted upon an able seaman in a vessel of war would break his spirit down more than a flogging." —Richard Henry Dana, Jr., *Two Years Before the Mast*; "Capt. Merril has no mercy on a sojer and despises likewise one who is impertinent or out of place."—Edward Ely, *The Wanderings of Edward Ely*; "'Let go, aft!' shouts the Captain. 'Let go, an' haul in. Damn them for worthless sodjers, anyway!'"—David W. Bone, *The Brassbounder*; "It mattered little if they were sailors or sojers, the Mates would make seamen of them on the voyage."—Sir James Bisset, *Sail Ho!*

son of a sea-cook: *an unworthy person.* In the early days of sailing, food aboard ship (after weeks, perhaps months, at sea) was notoriously bad. Some of the dissatisfaction felt by the crew would naturally be directed toward the cook—a person often already looked down upon as being next to useless. "Back in the eighteenth century the prime qualification for a cook was the loss of a hand or foot, which meant that a seaman could no longer work aloft and had to be found another job."—Joan Druett, *Hen Frigates*; "…one of the party, after denouncing him as a lying old son of a sea-cook who begrudged a fellow a few hours' liberty, exclaimed with an oath, 'But you don't bounce me out of my liberty, old chap...'"—Herman Melville, *Typee*; "Our one woe was our Cockney cook...He was, in truth, an outcast, heartily damned for spoiling our already miserable food."—John Cameron, *John Cameron's Odyssey*; "'...I'll choke the gizzard out of any cockeyed son of a sea cook who paints underneath a lifeboat in future without easing her out of the chocks.'"—Sir James Bisset, *Sail Ho!*

S O S: *a distress signal; a call for help.* This readily recognized call for help was officially adopted in 1908, initially for use at sea. The letters are neither an acronym nor an abbreviation, but were chosen because of their simplicity (dot dot dot, dash dash dash, dot dot dot) to send and receive in Morse Code.

sound to the kelson: *solid, dependable.* A kelson, or keelson, is a timber bolted parallel to the keel for added strength. "He was now once more happy in the affection of his shipmates, who, one and all, pronounced him sound to the kelson."—Herman Melville, *Omoo*

speak: *to hail and communicate with another ship at sea.* This curious use of the verb is more or less self-explanatory. "One of the incidents usually connected with 'gamming' and which never lost its interesting excitement to me, although witnessed many times, was the operation of 'speaking a ship' both being under sail at the time."—William Fish Williams, quoted in *One Whaling Family*; "We set our colors, as we were to windward of the *Gosnold*, which in the language of the sea indicated that we wished to speak her...."—ibid.; "On July 16 the wind was northwest and clear, the sea smooth, and a large bark, hull down, came in sight on the lee bow, and at 2:30 P.M. I spoke the stranger."—Joshua Slocum, *Sailing Alone Around the World*

splice hands: *shake hands.* Splicing (joining together) ropes, sheets, and cables, was an almost daily activity on sailing ships. "'What say ye, men, will ye splice hands on it, now? I think ye do look brave.'"—Herman Melville, *Moby Dick*

splice the mainbrace: *to give out grog; drink.* The origin of this expression is uncertain but may have to do with the strengthening ("bracing") effects of grog. "While the pumping and bailing was going on and all hands were struggling for their lives, the order was repeatedly given to 'splice the mainbrace'; that is to say, an abundant supply of grog was served out to cheer the sinking spirits of the men and stimulate them to renewed exertions."—Daniel Weston Hall, *Arctic Rovings*; "'Well, maties,' said one of them, at last—'I spose we shan't see each other again:—come, let's splice the main-brace all round, and drink to *the last voyage!*'"—Herman Melville, *Redburn*; "That evening in the dog watch, to celebrate our victory, all hands were called aft to 'splice the main brace,' and under the stimulating effects of the ardent spirits doled out we completely forgot for the time being the hardships we had suffered during the past three weeks."—Frederick Perry, *Fair Winds & Foul*

split on a rock: *be destroyed; come to grief.* Many a ship has split up upon hitting a rock. "He fancied, that if a sea-officer dressed well, and conversed genteelly, he would abundantly uphold the honor of his flag, and immortalize the tailor that made him. On that rock many young gentlemen split."—Herman Melville, *White-Jacket*

spotted dog: *a flour pudding, containing raisins, steamed or boiled in a cloth bag.* The raisins gave the pudding its fanciful resemblance to a white dog with black spots. "Sometimes I would instruct the steward to let them have a few raisins for their Sunday duff, out of my private stores; that was greatly appreciated—baked in a shallow tin it was irreverently called 'spotted dog.'"—W.H. Angel, *The Clipper Ship "Sheila"*

spouter: *a whaling ship.* (Whales spout.) This was a derogatory term. Whalers and the whalemen who sailed in them were often held in low regard by other seamen. "A spouter we knew her to be, by her cranes and boats and by her stump topgallant masts, and a certain slovenly look to her sails."—Richard Henry Dana, Jr., *Two Years Before the Mast*

square away: *to put in order.* The nautical meaning is "to square the yards [spars at right angles to masts] of a sailing vessel." "I was not going to miss a chance like this presented, to make westing after the rebuffs we had lately experienced, so we squared away."— W.H. Angel, *The Clipper Ship "Sheila"*

standby: *someone or something that can always be depended on.* From a ship being ready, i.e., standing by. "He came back in time for supper, very jubilant, saying that two engraving establishments were looking for a man and he was advised to stand by ready for a call."— Frederick Pease Harlow, *The Making of a Sailor*; "'I'll stand by,' the tugmaster sings out. 'Ye're in no condition to be on the high seas, Cap'n, and ye won't make port in this coming gale.'"—Sir James Bisset, *Sail Ho!*; "The watch on deck spent most of their time 'standing by' on the poop…"—William H. S. Jones, *The Cape Horn Breed*

stand watch: *to be on (guard duty).* "Watches" are the periods of time into which the day aboard a ship is divided.

steer clear of: *to avoid.* Shoals, sandbars, and derelict vessels are just a few examples of objects to steer clear of.

St. Elmo's fire: *the bluish electrical glow that appears on masts and other parts of a ship during storms at sea.* Also called *corposant* (from the Latin meaning "holy body") or *corpse light.* St. Elmo is the patron saint of sailors. "…they saw a flame at the mainmast which greatly upset the crew who called it 'St. Elmo's Fire.' It was believed to be a spirit and foretold a deadly storm."—Horace P. Beck, *The Folklore of Maine*; "…each yardarm was capped by the corpse candle of the old navigators, the 'corposant,' those weird and ghastly balls of fire whose shadow sailors believed foretold death." —Thomas Garry Fraser, *Captain Fraser's Voyages*; "I endeavored to give a plain philosophical reason for the appearance of the 'corpse lights,' but 'positive, electric matter' & 'friction' were words that did not occur in their dictionaries…"—Enoch

Carter Cloud, *Enoch's Voyage: Life on a Whale Ship*; "To make things more eerie, on the yards glittered bulbs of light, known to the sailors as corposants, but more correctly called St. Elmo's fire."—John Cameron, *John Cameron's Odyssey*

stem to stern: *from one end to the other.* A stem is a curved beam at the front of a ship forming part of the bow. The stern is the rear of the ship. "After coffee the decks were washed down from stem to stern, and all paint was wiped off with cotton swabs." —Frederick Perry, *Fair Winds & Foul*; "They were moored stem to stern in a grogshop, making a great noise, with a crowd of Indians and hungry half-breeds about them, and with a fair prospect of being stripped and dirked."—Richard Henry Dana, Jr., *Two Years Before the Mast*; "From stem to stern there was no shelter from the growing fury of the gale; but still the Old Man held to his course…"—David W. Bone, *The Brassbounder*

swallow the anchor: *to retire from (or quit) sailing.* This expression, obviously metaphorical, may (or may not) have been inspired by the nautical meaning of the noun *swallow*: the channel through which a rope runs in a block or mooring chock. "I can truthfully say that at no time of my misery did I wish to be ashore, or think of 'swallowing the anchor.'"—Thomas Garry Fraser, *Captain Fraser's Voyages*; "The Pilot grins again, thinking maybe of his own experiences, before he 'swallowed part of the anchor.'"—David W. Bone, *The Brassbounder*; "I thought that if only they'd turn around and come back…I'd have swallowed the anchor then and there—but they didn't come back!"—Sir James Bisset, *Sail Ho!*

swallow the hand-spike: *to desert ship.* The origin of this expression is unclear. Perhaps it is a humorous variation of "swallow the anchor."

sweep: *a long oar.* So called because of the sweeping motion used in rowing. "Fishing gear was scattered about the deck, long oars or sweeps and a mess of junk that might have been the accumulation of ages."—William Fish Williams, quoted in *One Whaling Family*; "She is no doubt a slaver from her very look, and her motion may easily be accounted for when we recollect that these vessels in time of danger employ sweeps to propel their vessel, worked by the miserable captives on board."—Edward Ely, *The Wanderings of Edward Ely*; "They were propelled by sweeps and manned by Chileans and beachcombers…"—Sir James Bisset, *Sail Ho!*

T

take in tow: *take charge of; take into one's care*. Ships "in tow" are drawn along by another vessel. "When the anchor was up the steam tug took us in tow and threaded her way out to sea in an almost incredible manner."—Edward Lacey, quoted in *Diaries from the Days of Sail*; "So I told him that if he would have a tug on hand to take the vessel in tow the minute the last piece of lumber was out of there I'd go."—George Fred Tilton, *"Cap'n George Fred" Himself*; "She evidently knew her man and took him in tow, leaving me aground on the corner, so I made my way back to the ship alone and turned in for the night."—Frederick Pease Harlow, *The Making of a Sailor*

take the wind out of one's sails: *to weaken or slow the progress of an adversary or rival*. A ship getting to windward of another ship (thus blocking the wind) would be said to take the wind out of its sails. "This so completely took the wind out of my sails that for a moment I could not answer."—Albert Sonnichsen, *Deep Sea Vagabonds*; "The big black side of the steamer to windward had taken the wind from our sails and we were blanketed."—Frederick Pease Harlow, *The Making of a Sailor*; "But it was the words of the song that struck us full in the face, taking the wind out of our sails and setting us both aback."—Frederick Pease Harlow, *The Making of a Sailor*

taken aback: *surprised; dumbfounded*. The wind blowing on the wrong side of all the sails at once—a dangerous circumstance—led to this expression. "We hauled up the trysail and courses, squared the after yards, and waited for the change, which came with a vengeance, from the northwest, the opposite point of the compass. Owing to our precautions, we were not taken aback, but ran before the wind with square yards." —Richard Henry Dana, Jr., *Two Years Before the Mast*; "I was so 'taken aback' by this intimation that for a moment I could make no reply."—ibid.; "…he was out again, singing out to clear up the royals, when they had not been set all day, ordering the helmsman to luff, when the sails were already shaking in the wind, and then the ship was taken aback, and Mr. Bishop was obliged to take the command…a drunken captain is more to be feared than to be pitied."—Edward Ely, *The Wanderings of Edward Ely*; "Bursting upon them, I took them completely aback, so little had they imagined I could escape."—John Cameron, *John Cameron's Odyssey*

tap the admiral (also **suck the monkey**): *to drink illicitly*. Sailors were often forbidden to purchase liquor while ashore in the tropics. To evade this regulation, they would fill empty coconuts with rum and drink from them with a straw (as if drinking the coconut milk).

tar: *a sailor*. The term may be a shortening of "tarpaulin," a canvas waterproofed with tar and used as a protective covering against moisture. Or it may have its origin in the practice by sailors of applying a coating of tar to their clothing (and even their hair) as a means of weatherproofing. "Our tars are having a holy day, and they have enjoyed it like sensible men, in drying their wet clothes, bedding etc."—Edward Ely, *The Wanderings of Edward Ely*; "The salts at the time wore their hair in pigtails…to keep hair out of one's eyes when working aloft, the pigtails were coated with tar."—James Clary, *Superstitions of the Sea*; "But in order to be a successful navigator or sailor it is not necessary to hang a tar-bucket about one's neck."—Joshua Slocum, *Sailing Alone Around the World*; "I am a sailor and a descendant of a race of sailors, and as they used to express it of my kind in olden times, every hair on my head is a rope-yarn, and every drop of my blood is Stockholm tar."—W.H. Angel, *The Clipper Ship "Sheila"*

tarpaulin muster: *a general contribution by a group of sailors for a worthy cause.* In this sense *tarpaulin* may simply be slang for *sailor*, or may refer to the sailors' waterproof headgear (so that the expression is equivalent to the landsman's "pass the hat"). "When we heard of her misfortune and her great longing to return home, we made a tarpaulin muster, bought her a ticket to Scotland, escorted her to one of the Western Ocean ferryboats, and sent her off rejoicing, though tearful at parting from us."—John Cameron, *John Cameron's Odyssey*; "For the new arrival we made a tarpaulin muster, to which the crew contributed a tidy sum."—ibid.

tarred with the same brush (or **stick**): *alike.* A coating of tar makes everyone look alike. "Many natives, many foreigners, be their stratum of society high or low, were tarred with the same brush."—John Cameron, *John Cameron's Odyssey*; "He only thinks of leaving no 'holidays' (places not tarred), for in case he should, he would have to go over the whole again; or of dropping no tar upon the deck, for then there would be a soft word in his ear from the mate."—Richard Henry Dana, Jr., *Two Years Before the Mast*; "Our men have been engaged in setting up the standing rigging, and they are as black as coal heaves with the tar which has fried out of the ropes."—Edward Ely, *The Wanderings of Edward Ely*

Tell that to the marines! *a retort expressing skepticism, as if to say, "Do you expect me to believe that?"* From the low regard in which marines (troops stationed on board ships) were often held by sailors. As landsmen, marines would be unskilled in the ways of the sea, and thus looked down upon as clumsy or ignorant. The antagonism felt by sailors might also have resulted in part from the perception that the troops stationed aboard ship were idle loafers, or perhaps from the fact that the soldiers were sometimes called upon to discipline unruly seamen. "Marine is the term applied more particularly to a man who is ignorant and clumsy about seaman's work—a greenhorn, a landlubber." —Richard Henry Dana, Jr., *Two Years Before the Mast*; "'Tell that to the marines,' the Captain growled."—Sir James Bisset, *Sail Ho!*

tender: *coal-car; a railroad car attached to the rear of a locomotive for the purpose of carrying fuel and water.* A small vessel that serves as auxiliary and store-ship to a larger one, or one that ferries supplies between ship and shore.

Thar she blows! *(The whaleman's cry that a whale has been sighted.)* When a whale blows, or spouts mist (water and air), it betrays its presence to the watchful whalemen. Similar cries are "Thar she breaches!" and "Thar she white-waters!" "'There-re-re she blows!' aroused all hands from the contagious lethargy into which we had fallen, and few moments sufficed to show us a fine Sperm Whale!" —Enoch Carter Cloud, *Enoch's Voyage: Life on a Whale Ship*; "The cry was always 'There blows,' with the last word long drawn out and, as the spouts continued, simply the word 'Blows' is cried with each spout."—William Fish Williams, quoted in *One Whaling Family*; "'There she blows! there! there! there! she blows! she blows!'"—Herman Melville, *Moby Dick*

the coast is clear: *it's okay to act; there are no witnesses or obstacles.* The term was probably made popular by smugglers.

The smoking lamp is lit. *Permission is given to smoke.* When the custom of smoking tobacco came into fashion in the sixteenth century, ships (the wooden vessels themselves, their cargoes, and especially the gunpowder stored aboard) were highly flammable. The smoking lamp was introduced as a safety measure; when lit, it indicated that smoking was allowed at the time in that place (generally near the galley or forecastle) and provided—in the days before matches or cigarette lighters—a convenient means of igniting a pipe. "They would sit on their chests…eyeing the forecastle lamp, at which they had lighted so many a pleasant pipe."—Herman Melville, *Redburn*

three sheets in (or **to**) **the wind**: *drunk; intoxicated.* When tacking, a full-rigger is essentially disabled (moving erratically downwind) when sails are helplessly shaking in the wind. This can happen when sheets (ropes) are not properly attached. The following gives a graphic description of the type of circumstance that no doubt inspired the metaphor: "'Let go the sheets!' the Mate roared…a 'sheet' being a manila or wire rope or chains secured to the lower corners of sails…but in the violent gusts the flapping and slatting of the released sails threatened to pull the masts and yards down to crash on our heads, and the sheets flailed the deck like giant whiplashes…"—Sir James Bisset, *Sail Ho!*; "He talked a great deal about propriety and steadiness, and gave good advice to the youngsters…but seldom went up to the town without coming down 'three sheets in the wind.'"—Richard Henry Dana, Jr., *Two Years Before the Mast*; "6 PM Came aboard, and found a portion of the watch '3 sheets in the wind & to her fluttering!'"—Enoch Carter Cloud, *Enoch's Voyage: Life on a Whale Ship*; "Sheets are *not* sails, as some poets would have us believe."—Hiram P. Bailey, *Shanghaied out of 'Frisco in the 'Nineties*; "But he fell; he got into some of the wet goods one day and he came on deck with three sheets in the wind and the other shivering like the devil."—George Fred Tilton, *"Cap'n George Fred" Himself*; "We were no exception to thousands of other sailors and by the time the ship was made fast to the dock our men, who had sworn, time and again, that not another drop of whiskey should ever pass their lips again, threw their good resolutions to the wind at the smell of the 'knock-out-drops' and half of the crew were 'three sheets in the wind' before we passed under the Brooklyn Bridge."—Frederick Pease Harlow, *The Making of a Sailor*

tide over: *to support (financially) through a difficult period.* The term comes from the practice of getting a deep draught vessel over a sandbar or shoal by taking advantage of high tide.

tip the fin: *shake hands.* A fin on a fish is like a hand on a person.

touch and go: *risky; a precarious situation.* A ship in shallow water or near rocks may touch bottom or objects as it moves along. Another explanation is that a ship may touch (at port) then immediately leave (go).

trimmer: *a person who changes opinion (more specifically, political sides) to suit the needs of the moment.* To trim sails is to adjust them to take advantage of the wind. A mariner who constantly trimmed his sails to take advantage of every little puff would be termed a "trimmer."

turn in all standing: *to go to bed with one's clothes on.* "Turn in" refers to swinging into one's bunk. "All standing" means with all sails set. "After we had got below, some of the watch lighted their pipes to have a smoke before turning in, as seamen express it."— Lewis E. Lovell, *Stories of Yarmouth Shipmasters*; "...and the starboard watch goes off duty for the afternoon 'turn in'—the expression 'going to bed' is never heard at sea."—W.H. Angel, *The Clipper Ship "Sheila"*; "All but the 'turning out,' or rising from your berth when the watch was called at night—*that* I never fancied."—Herman Melville, *Redburn*; "We turned in day after day with clothes steaming wet and turned out with them still steaming, and all this in intense cold."—John Cameron, *John Cameron's Odyssey*; "South'ard of the 'forties' Old Jock slept 'all standing,' as we say."—David W. Bone, *The Brassbounder*; "The blankets, too, were hard with salt, and blackened with coal-dust and dirt ground into them by the heavy boots of men who had turned into their bunks 'all standing', to thaw out or snatch an hour's sleep before Eight Bells again called them on deck."—William H.S. Jones, *The Cape Horn Breed*

U

uncharted waters: *the unknown; uncertainty (with the implication of possible danger)*. Navigators have always depended on charts to warn them of hazards, such as rocks or hidden shoals. In the early days of sailing much of the world's ocean was uncharted.

under the weather: *feeling sick or unwell*. The term may derive from the fact that a person feeling the effects of bad weather at sea tends to seek shelter under the weather bulwarks. Or it may simply derive from the more literal meaning of being exposed to bad weather. "On coming up close I found that it was my old friend, Captain Casey, of the *Margaret and Peggy*, who was, as it were, slightly under the weather owing to having a cargo of rum on board."— John Kenlon, *Fourteen Years A Sailor*

V

veer away: *to swerve; change direction.* A ship "veers away" by turning away from the direction of the wind. *Veer* with this meaning derives from Latin through French. The strictly nautical term, to **veer**, meaning to slacken, release, or let out (a line or anchor) is an entirely different word, derived from Dutch. "We lost much time daily by veering away to pump ship, which was obligatory if the precious cargo was to be kept from damage."—Thomas Garry Fraser, *Captain Fraser's Voyages*; "…wind and sea increased to such an extent that I insisted we depart while we could, the breeze having veered and now affording us an excellent slant."—John Cameron, *John Cameron's Odyssey*

W

walk the plank: *to be executed at sea by being led blindfolded along a plank that extends over the side of the ship.* This form of execution was practiced by pirates. "If you get into the stores again and I learn of it, by God, I'll make you walk the plank!"—John Cameron, *John Cameron's Odyssey*

waster: *spendthrift; prodigal; idle, useless fellow.* The word is a misspelling of "waister," a sailor who was assigned to the middle part (waist) of the ship. In the days of press gangs, when men were forced against their will to serve on ships, many unskilled hands were taken aboard. Until they became more experienced, they were assigned menial tasks such as sweeping the decks, which required little or no skill. "Then there are the *Waisters*...These fellows are all Jimmy Duxes—sorry chaps, who never put foot in ratlin, or venture above the bulwarks. Inveterate '*sons of farmers*,' with the hay-seed yet in their hair, they are consigned to the congenial superintendence of the chicken-coops, pig-pens, and potato-lockers. These are generally placed amidships...They are the tag-rag and bob-tail of the crew; and he who is good for nothing else is good enough for a *Waister*."—Herman Melville, *White-Jacket*

wear ship: *to turn the ship around before the wind, keeping the sails full; to come about with the stern to windward.* The following nicely describes this: "On the other hand an attempt to wear the ship—

that is, to turn her about away from the wind and get her on the other tack, with her other side exposed to the storm—also might be signally disastrous. All of us were called aft to decide what should be done. Most were in favor of trying to wear the vessel rather than awaiting better weather."—John Cameron, *John Cameron's Odyssey*; "'Out there, the watch! Turn out!' in tone that admits no protest. 'Turn out, damn ye, an' stand-by t' wear ship!'"—David W. Bone, *The Brassbounder*; "In the meantime, the captain had again wore ship and we were circling around the disabled boats."—Frederick Pease Harlow, *The Making of a Sailor*

whistle for a breeze: *whistle to make the wind blow.* Although it was considered bad luck to whistle while on board ship (to do so would surely bring on a hurricane or at the least a gale), during periods of prolonged calm a captain or mate might whistle, in order to bring on sufficient winds to fill the sails. "I had often heard that old sailors wouldn't allow any whistling on board ship, for they were a superstitious set and claimed that any whistling would certainly bring on a gale, followed by bad luck; but whistling for a breeze on Long Island Sound, I concluded, must be different."—Frederick Pease Harlow, *The Making of a Sailor*; "The captain, a firm believer in old superstitions, whistled softly at intervals for a wind and took due credit for his efforts when a breeze sometimes came in answer to his summons."—Sir James Bisset, *Sail Ho!*; "Whistle, sailor, whistle for a wind!"—William H. S. Jones, *The Cape Horn Breed*

white ash breeze: *(a humorous reference to) the power supplied by rowing.* Oars are often made from the sturdy wood of the white ash tree. Also simply **ash breeze** (sometimes in the adjectival sense of *becalmed*). "...the three mates stood up proudly, occasionally backing the after oarsman with an exhilarating cry of, 'There she slides, now! Hurrah for the white-ash breeze!'"—Herman Melville, *Moby Dick*

wing and wing: *with sails extended on both sides.* The metaphor comparing sails to wings is an ancient one. "...the ships had spread their white wings and flown; the wharves were desolate."—Lafcadio Hearn, *Fantastics and Other Fancies*; "We spread the 'Sheila's' wings once more; though this time loaded under my personal supervision, I was sorry to find we were trimmed by the head, and drawing sixteen feet aft, and seventeen feet, nine inches forward..."—W.H. Angel, *The Clipper Ship "Sheila"*

with flying colors: *with great success.* A victorious ship enters port with all flags (colors) flying.

wood and black skin: *being so close to a whale that the boat touches it.* "The boat being, in whaling parlance, 'wood and black skin' i.e. the wood of the boat touching the skin of the whale, by reaching over I could have placed my hand upon one, when the mate shouted to let him have it."—John Wetherell, *The Adventures of John Wetherell*

Y

Yo heave ho!: *Pull together!* or *Give a hard push!* To heave is to raise or lift with a strenuous effort. The rhythm of the expression mimics the rhythm of the task being performed, or the motion of the ship. "I remembered the *yo heave ho!* of the sailors, as they just showed their woolen caps above the high bulwarks."—Herman Melville, *Redburn*; "...the creaking of the spars and the flapping of sails mingling with the hoarse shouting and 'ho heave a ho's' of the crew seemed to breathe out a grand requiem mass for the peaceful repose of the departed soul."—Frederick Perry, *Fair Winds & Foul*; "And amid these goodly yo-heave-ho'ers the commander must perforce sit, doubtless endeavoring to dismiss from his mind the insinuating thought that on the high seas he holds the power of life and death."—Cornelia Otis Skinner, "The Captain's Table"; "Oh! you can't go wrong in a nautical song, / If you sing yoe, ho, lads, oh!"—W.H. Angel, *The Clipper Ship "Sheila"*; "Boats were flying to and fro like fury, windlasses were clacking, seamen were chaunting their yo-heave-oh."—John Wetherell, *The Adventures of John Wetherell*

About the Author

E DWARD LODI is no mere **figurehead**. Though no **old salt**, he's an experienced **shellback** when it comes to the use of words. He **knows his ropes, from stem to stern**. Don't be **taken aback** if he **takes the wind out of your sails**, then **takes you in tow**. He possesses an MA in English Literature from Boston University and has taught English at Shaw University and at the Massachusetts Maritime Academy. He is the author of fourteen books, and over the years has published dozens of articles and essays pertaining to language and literature. He is currently **at the helm** (Editor in chief) at Rock Village Publishing.

About the Artist

ROBERT **D**UFF receives his artistic inspiration from everyday life—a commonplace that's often overlooked in busy times. He creates paintings that have feelings of serenity, such as 19th-century lighthouses against a brilliant sunset or a delicately woven Nantucket basket filled with hydrangeas. He developed his techniques from extensive studies of the 19th-century American Painters of the Hudson River and Luminous schools. His thirty-five-year career has brought a unique maturity and vision to his work. He is accomplished both as a landscape and still-life painter, and his work shows an acute understanding of color and light.

Born in New Bedford, Massachusetts, Robert Duff grew up in nearby Acushnet and spent his childhood in what he calls "a Norman Rockwell painting." Long summer days spent wandering the shores of the Acushnet River or playing in fields of freshly mowed hay left him with a deep respect and admiration for natural beauty. "These memories, perhaps larger than life, are often the catalyst for many of my most popular paintings. I want to bring you where I have been."

Together with his wife, Debra, he established the Duff Gallery in 1986. Their personal style of working directly with clients has given them great pleasure in seeing his work acquired by both private and corporate collectors worldwide.

The Duff Gallery
Whaling National Historical Park
36 North Water Street
New Bedford, Massachusetts 02740
phone: 508.993.3200
online gallery: www.robertduff.com